BLOSSOMS AND
BROKEN FLOWERS

Selected writings from High Peaks Pure Earth

TIBET
RELIEF FUND

First published 2019 by Tibet Relief Fund, 2 Baltic Place, 287 Kingsland Road, London, N1 5AQ, UK

www.tibetrelieffund.co.uk

ISBN 978-1-999-3673-0-5

Collated and edited by Dechen Pemba

Design and line illustrations by Nyima Stewart

Printed in India by Norbu Graphics
1/6, Basement, Vikram Vihar
Lajpat Nagar - IV, New Delhi -110024, India

CONTENTS

TIBET
RELIEF FUND

tibetrelieffund.co.uk

@tibetrelieffund

INTRODUCTION FROM TIBET RELIEF FUND

Tibet Relief Fund seeks to preserve and promote the great variety of Tibet's cultural heritage and is committed to amplifying and celebrating Tibetan voices around the world.

We are therefore delighted to be working with High Peaks Pure Earth to publish these selected works from their website. By translating writings from within Tibet and the People's Republic of China, accompanied by discerning commentary, High Peaks Pure Earth presents a unique and vital insight into Tibet today. The site provides a platform for a fascinating and diverse selection of voices; Tibet Relief Fund is proud to have this opportunity to publish this vibrant, contemporary and honest insight into life in 21st century Tibet.

In April 2017 High Peaks Pure Earth carried out a readers' survey. A common theme in responses from its Tibetan audience was the significance of the link the website creates between the global Tibetan community in exile and their brothers and sisters still living inside Tibet. The ever-increasing ubiquity of internet access has enabled this valuable picture of modern Tibet to be shared around the world, transcending the barriers of language and censorship.

With this publication, Tibet Relief Fund aims to further expand this access by distributing copies of these selected writings to students in the older years of the Tibetan schools we work with in India and Nepal. After nearly 70 years of occupation, we hope this book can play a part in bolstering the sense of connection between Tibet and the younger generations of the exile community.

London
21 November 2018

Tibet Relief Fund   tibetrelieffund.co.uk

རི་མཐོ་ས་གཙང་། | high peaks pure earth | 高峰净土

INTRODUCTION TO THE SELECTION
Dechen Pemba

The writings in this booklet comprise highlights selected from the website High Peaks Pure Earth which was started towards the end of 2008.

During and after the 2008 Tibetan uprising I noticed a lack of attention being paid to voices on the ground that were writing online. Tibetan blogs were a valuable information source in 2008 but difficult to access for several reasons, the main being they were written in Tibetan or Chinese but also because of internet censorship. In particular, the blog by Tsering Woeser played, and continues to play, a key role in understanding Tibet today.

Therefore, High Peaks Pure Earth started as a project to make those voices on the ground more accessible through good quality translations and to give commentary by providing context and analysis. From starting with translations of blog posts, we have since expanded to translating poetry, interviews and music videos, as well as hosting book reviews, guest posts and book recommendations.

The phrase High Peaks Pure Earth is lifted from a manuscript from the 9th century which reads "The heart of the world / fenced around by snow / The headland of all rivers / Where the mountains are high and the land is pure". It is a phrase as ancient as written Tibetan and, as far as we know, marks the first time that we Tibetans wrote about and reflected on ourselves.

My aim for High Peaks Pure Earth is to stay abreast of Tibetan cultural production and to keep translating thought-provoking writings and highlight popular cultural pieces and accompanying discussions. It is important to place the voices from Tibetans inside Tibet and the People's Republic of China firmly inside the narrative of Tibet today, amplifying our own stories and experiences.

As a web-based project monitoring blogs and social media, this is the first time that writings from High Peaks Pure Earth have been published in book form. I am thrilled that readers who might not have had regular internet access can now read the writings and hopefully feel a connection with Tibet in a new and different way. Thank you to Tibet Relief Fund for their support in realising this book.

London
18 November 2018

Dechen Pemba
Editor
High Peaks Pure Earth   highpeakspureearth.com

Tsering Woeser in Lhasa. April 2018

TSERING WOESER ON HIGH PEAKS PURE EARTH
Tsering Woeser

For reasons we all know, for a long time it has been difficult for the voices of Tibetans to be heard in the wider world, the machinery of the state controls all aspects of information and suppresses, alters and substitutes. However, the emergence of the internet has opened up a space for voices fighting to be heard, and has also created a bridge of communication and exchange between Tibet and the rest of the world.

High Peaks Pure Earth is exactly this kind of bridge.

High Peaks Pure Earth is the first blog devoted to translating the voices of Tibetans inside Tibet and the People's Republic of China into English, it was founded in a critical year in Tibet's history, 2008. More importantly, High Peaks Pure Earth translates Tibetan voices regardless of whether they write in Tibetan or Chinese and through High Peaks Pure Earth, more people can become familiar with the situation in Tibet today, what Tibetans are thinking about and their activities.

My blog is considered to be a very important blog, not only because it was the first in Tibet written by a dissident or intellectual but also, because it is written in Chinese, it is considered to be an influential blog in the Chinese language world. I am grateful to High Peaks Pure Earth for the many articles on my blog they have translated into English, and the section on High Peaks Pure Earth which is dedicated solely to my writings.

I believe there will be many more Tibetan blogs written in Tibetan or Chinese in the future and High Peaks Pure Earth will continue to introduce them to the world. It goes without saying that this also needs the world's support.

Beijing
22 December 2010

Tsering Woeser

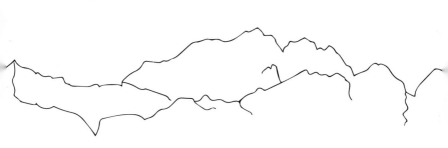

2008 AND POST-2008
ཕྱི་ལོ་2008་སྔ་རྗེས།

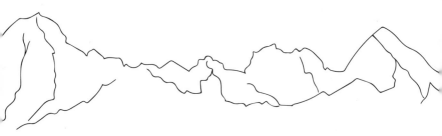

THEY
Jamyang Kyi

They constantly tried to use various methods to make me betray others. During that time, one scene from "The Lives of Others" occurred to me from time to time. The woman in the film, after endlessly suffering unimaginable degrees of intimidation and atrocity, loses herself and turns her back on her beloved man. When the man stares at her with a sense of disbelief, unable to bear her feelings, she runs into the road in front of an oncoming vehicle. There, she ends her blooming beauty and precious life. Though it has been over two years since I saw the film, I cannot forget the depth of frustration in the man's stare and the aggrieved look on the woman's face. Today, these images from the film appear even more real in my mind.

My heart cracked like a dried-out riverbank with feelings of sadness, hopelessness, frustration and anger. And I longed for the moisture of light rain. One evening when I was tied to that chair again, I heard the sound of religious songs of a melancholic nature. I realised that this was the first time I was hearing the sound of a living being. This was soothing medicine for my bleeding heart. Since then, I began paying attention to this prayer-tune and awaiting it with hope each day. At that mosque, the devout practitioner prayed four to five times every day. Normally that prayer-tune could have been perceived as being unpleasant, but during those days it became the best medicine to revive my spirit. For that, I'm deeply grateful to the mosque and practitioner. If ever a day comes for me to get out, I swore to myself that I would pay a visit to the mosque. Even today, that wish hasn't disappeared from my heart.

In a magazine there is an oil painting of a landscape that I have looked at countless times. In the painting there is a lone cottage of European style that stands by a lake. That was the only home in the wide, hilly grassland. It afforded me a sense of tranquility and peace. Imagining that house to be my own family home, I began to visualise my two daughters playing chase in the grassy meadow near the house; my husband cutting grass beside the lake and I myself, busily cooking dinner awaiting the return of the cattle. That, too, became a means to console and revive my shattered spirit.

One day, as soon as the protests first began, my husband said with a sigh, "Those who have died are already gone. But those who have been arrested are certain to be cast into the 18 realms of hell and bound to suffer immeasurably." On the other hand, empathising with those who had died and their bereaved and loved ones, I was deeply touched and moved to endless tears of sympathy. And at the time, I could not fully comprehend the implications of the incident in which three Tibetans had leapt to their death from a roof top.

Each interrogation session aroused a different kind of fear in me. One day in the middle of an interrogation, I thought instead of enduring this, it would be better to be killed by a single bullet. My family and relatives would grieve but as for me, I would have to suffer the pain only once. One day when I was in the washroom, out of nowhere, I found myself thinking about the means or methods of taking my own life. Those days I remembered the small knife that was confiscated at Zhihu Hotel. They hadn't seen another small knife that was in my handbag during the search. When the chief interrogator asked why I kept a small knife, I replied that it was for eating fruit. But on the other hand there is a small story about this small knife.

Ever since the Chinese-Tibetan conflict had flared up, and as result of the government's deliberate propaganda, the Chinese would stare at Tibetans with hatred, whether it be in a bus, the market place or on any public road. Once, when I was walking down the road with my daughter, who was wearing the traditional chuba that my friend Walza Norzin Wangmo had bought her as a gift, a Chinese kid of about six or seven years old came yelling in front of my daughter and stood blocking her way. This kind of Chinese attitude wasn't an isolated incident that we experienced but rather the common experience of other Tibetans too. So, for self-defence I had bought another small knife. Later, on reflection, I felt relief that I hadn't had the chance to get hold of those two knives. Otherwise, during an interrogation session, under unbearable torture, I would have frantically searched my pouch and then stared at the blue veins of my left wrist. Were I to get hold of the knife then, I would surely have cut the veins of my wrist.

During those days, Wang Lixong's essay on the stages of suicide came to mind from time to time. And it was a completely different feeling from when I had first read it. I realised for the first time how difficult and harsh it is to betray and deceive someone. I felt that I could understand him now that I could understand it myself.

During those days when I was thrown in front of the six gates of hell, the person I thought of most was my kind and dear mother. Although it has been nearly three years since she passed away, she is very much alive in my heart. What is comforting is the realisation that my dear mother has already left me. Otherwise, if she were alive and to witness my incarceration in prison, I know she would go insane.

At the height of unbearable torture, usually I invoked the names of my mother and Goddess Tara for protection. One afternoon when I was tied to a stool, everyone left for lunch except for one female secret police officer. For many days, I had suppressed my tears of suffering silently. But at that moment of weakness, I could not bear it any longer and cried out "Mother, Mother". The longing for my mother grew more intense and the suffering worsened, and I sobbed. As I was sobbing with pain, all my limbs went numb. At that time the fat man came and said, "You're crying intentionally because you know I'm here." Pressing his finger to my forehead, he warned, "If you continue to wail, I will stop this interrogation."

He shouted in a loud voice, "Are you this stubborn because you think we are making a false accusations?" and left the room. Although it was not something that I was doing intentionally, being aware of his presence there, I still couldn't stop crying. At the time, the nerves in both my hands turned stiff and I couldn't unclench my fist when I tried to force them open. A long time passed sobbing, with my entire body drenched in sweat…

September 2008

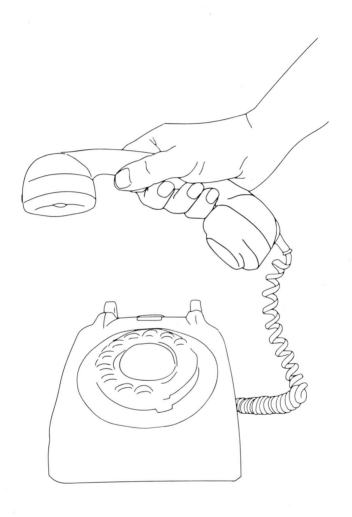

TELEPHONE RANG

Lhakyi

Lyrics: Tenzin Gyab
Composition: Denkhrug Dawoe

The telephone rang, the telephone rang
The phone call was from the peak of the Land of Snows
A whisper said that the Snowlion is to return
Let the people of the Land of Snows enjoy and celebrate!
Tibetans within and without Tibet will soon reunite

The telephone rang, the telephone rang
The phone call was from the dense forest
A whisper said that the Forest Tiger is to return
Let ruddy-faced Tibetans celebrate!
Tibetans within and without Tibet will soon reunite

The telephone rang, the telephone rang
The phone call was from central Tibet
A whisper said that His Holiness is to return
Let Tibetans from the three provinces enjoy and celebrate!
Tibetans within and without Tibet will soon reunite

Let Tibetans from the three provinces enjoy and celebrate!
Tibetans within and without Tibet will soon reunite

March 2010

THE SOUND OF UNITY

Sherten

Lyrics: Taglha Gye
Music: Dubey

Amdo, Kham and Ü-Tsang all belong to the same family
We have a common destiny

Let's all blossom together like flowers
Hand in hand in harmony

Hand in hand in harmony
Let's step forwards

If you care about the future of our nationality
All three provinces should unite

Amdo, Kham and Ü-Tsang all belong to the same family
We have a common destiny

Tibetans of the land of snows
Unite as one!

Amdo, Kham and Ü-Tsang all belong to the same family
We have a common destiny

Hand in hand in harmony
Let's step forwards

If we care about the well-being and the future of
our nationality who are in despair
People from Amdo, Kham and Ü-Tsang, hold hands
together in harmony, unite as one!

O Tibetans!
Unite, unite
If you think of the sadness on the face of your father

O Tibetans!
Unite, unite
If you think of the tears from the heart of your mother

O Tibetans!
Unite, unite
Tibetans of the Land of Snows unite

We are the kin of the same parentage
We are the inheritors of a nation
O ruddy-faced Tibetans

O Tibetans!
Unite, unite
If you think of the months and years of joys and sorrows

O Tibetans!
Unite, unite
Tibetans from all parts of the high plateau unite

O Tibetans!
Unite, unite
If you think of the vista of the Land of Snows

O Tibetans!
Unite, unite
Kindred, old or young, unite

We are the keepers of herds in the nomadic lands of the upper reaches
We are the farmers in the valleys of the low lying lands
O ruddy-faced Tibetans

O Tibetans!
Unite, unite
If you think of our destiny of tears and laughter

O Tibetans!
Unite, unite
Three provinces unite

O Tibetans!
Unite, unite
If you think of the peace and happiness of a life of freedom

O Tibetans!
Unite, unite
Young men and women unite

We are the messengers of the new era
We are the future inheritors of the land surrounded by snowy ranges
O ruddy-faced Tibetans

July 2010

MOURNING
Sengdor

The sadness of living is more painful than death
Unbearable sorrow turned you all into glowing red skeletons

The mouth quivers with flames
The hands are pierced with flames
Flames burn in the breast
Rosary beads of fire scatter to the ground

Look at the smoke rising
from the monastery's golden roof
Look at the doors of each monk's cell

In every moment
After a storm bursts on one grassland
Another storm bursts on the other grassland
Following the direction of the wind
Dark shadows move accordingly

Written on one night in October 2011

HELPLESS

Tsering Woeser

I take a book
Read a few pages and set it aside
Outside my window, Beijing
Filled with feelings of Doomsday
In the mists, I cannot see
Tall buildings not so very far away.
What really grabs me lies
Much further away,
Fearless clansmen,
Amidst the flames, will they be
Hit by red bullets?

17 January 2012

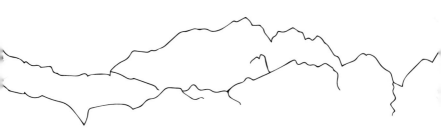

I AM TIBETAN

ང་བོད་པ་ཡིན།

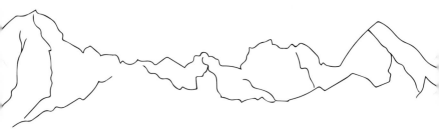

THE LHAKAR PLEDGE

I. The Nature of the Movement

This modest movement called Lhakar comes from the fact that I am Tibetan, and it is like a note reminding us that we are Tibetan in our daily life. Through this movement, we restore, renovate and keep our language, culture, identity and tradition.

Through this technique we can keep the soul language of the Snowland's people till the end of humankind. This technique helps us retain Tibetan culture, Tibetan good morals and the traditions which are born from our soul language. This technique is easy and it is meaningful.

2. Anticipation

This Lhakar movement began in anticipation as remedial medicine for hundreds of diseases for Tibetan brothers and sisters who live in every region. I hope that many Tibetan brothers and sisters will participate in this movement without any invitation and follow the eight promises or keep even one of them, and practice it. I am requesting all Tibetans to keep this pledge as I kneel down on my knees and humbly fold my hands on my chest, and make this request innumerable times.

Lhakar:

I am Tibetan, from today I will speak pure Tibetan in my family.
I am Tibetan, from today I will speak pure Tibetan whenever I meet a Tibetan.
I am Tibetan, from today I will remind myself every day that I am a Tibetan till I die.
I am Tibetan, from today I will wear only Tibetan traditional dress, chuba, every Wednesday.
I am Tibetan, from today I will speak only Tibetan every Wednesday.
I am Tibetan, from today I will learn Tibetan language.
I am Tibetan, from today I will stop eating meat and only eat a vegetarian diet and gain more merit every Wednesday.
I am Tibetan, from today I will only use Tibetan and speak Tibetan when I call or send a message to Tibetans.

June 2010

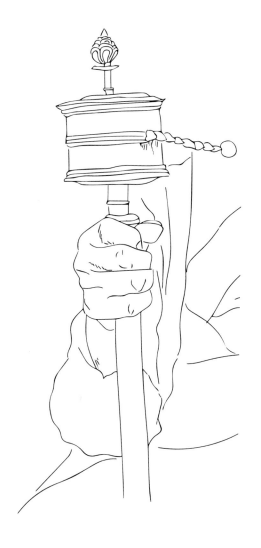

I AM TIBETAN
Khampa Snow

I am Tibetan
A black-haired and ochre-faced Tibetan
My feet have trod countless snowy peaks
In our proud realm of snowy extremes
Sincere smiles
Remain through summer rains and winter snows
Our will and grit shine yet through bitter cold and cruel heat

I am Tibetan
A compassionate-hearted Tibetan
Prayer wheels and beads have flown in my hand since time eternal
Our piety was cast in Shambala's pure lands
The six-syllable mantra is muttered
Under the discriminatory gaze of others and the ridicule of misunderstanding
We pray as ever for harmony and well-being for all living things

I am Tibetan
A Tibetan who can sing and dance
The seven colours of the rainbow are woven into my long flowing sleeves
And our jubilant dances raise the Yangtze and Yellow Rivers
Our innocent dances and
Songs of praise sound out in the golden era, delight dances through the soul

I am Tibetan
A dream-cherishing Tibetan
The wisdom and glory in the 30 letters of the Tibetan alphabet
Shine on the path of our progress
The milk of ten bright cultures
Fortifies our minds and bodies
With the blessings of our ancestors' culture we stagger out with leaps and
bounds into the ranks of the world

I am Tibetan
The agitated blood in my veins is a constant reminder
I am Tibetan
In my lilting mother tongue I want to say loudly
"I am Tibetan"

18 March 2010

I AM TIBETAN

Adong Paldothar

I feel
From the eternal transmigration and
Boundless mercy: treating all living creatures like one's own parents
That I am a Tibetan

I feel
From the truth of the light breeze touching my face
Caused by the fast-spinning prayer wheel in Grandma's hands
That I am a Tibetan

I feel
From the meditation of the Lamas
From their heavenly murmurs when praying for all living beings and world
peace
That I am a Tibetan

I feel
From our natural and harmonious coexistence with antelopes, condors, as well
as forests and springs
That I am a Tibetan

I feel
From the piety of honouring mines and riverheads as gods and spirits
Worshipping and caring for them
That I am a Tibetan

I feel
From the phrase we would say every time we dirty a small piece of crushed
food and throw it away:
"May it be picked up by a blind bird"
That I am a Tibetan

I feel
From all those innate ancient bearings
Such as spitting out then covering it with earth
That I am a Tibetan

I feel
From the maxims and idioms spoken and written in the great immortal
Tibetan language
That I am a Tibetan

I feel
From the glittering starry splendour in the sky above the Derge Scriptures
Printing Hall where the thirty ancient letters are preserved
That I am a Tibetan

I feel
From the Hor-Ling War, in which King Gesar's red-haired horse surpassed
Achilles' steed
And which is as immortal as the Trojan War
That I am a Tibetan

I feel
From the image of a foetus obtained through Tibetan medicine as accurate as a
contemporary ultrasound
The Tibetan tantra which explains the essence of life ?as well as the Tibetan
calendar which predicted the existence of water on the moon
That I am a Tibetan

I feel
From the curves of David Beckham's crossings
The big feet of Tibetan football players and
The highland gene of the Royal Polo Team
That I am a Tibetan

I feel
From the wedding between the monkey and the demoness
As well as the legend about the formation of the Plateau: first ocean, then
forest and finally grassland, of which Darwin only learned much later
That I am a Tibetan

I feel
From the yaks leisurely wandering in the frosty snow on the peak of the earth
The naked herd boys playing by the rivers under snow-covered mountains
And the pulse of the clan, whose ancestors used to steal and drink the milk of
Snowlions
That I am a Tibetan

I feel
From the invincible Tibetan Tsenpos (Kings) and the great changes from above
and below the Sakya, the Pamodrupa, as well as the Ganden Phodrang rule
That I am a Tibetan

I feel
From the documents written in Tibetan buried under the dunes of Dunhuang
The immortal colours of the Guge mural paintings and the towering Tibetan
stone houses on the Ancient Tea and Horse Caravan Road
That I am a Tibetan

I feel
From the entirety consisting of Ü-Tsang, the holy region of Buddhism
Dokham, the region of braves and beauties
And Amdo, the region of fine steeds
That I am a Tibetan

I feel
From the grey stone tablet under the white and red palaces of the Potala Palace
in memory of the Alliance
And the sKamalok" Clan of Dokham
That I am a Tibetan

I feel
From all the confusion and sullenness
Of not knowing but being Tibetan
That I am Tibetan

January 2010

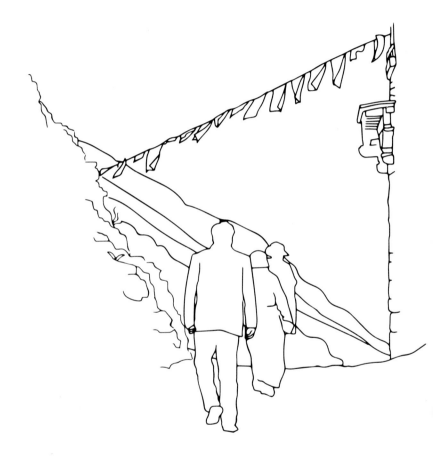

I AM TIBETAN
Gade Tsering

Because I'm Tibetan, every time I salute Mother Nature in awe:
The snow-covered mountains, the grasslands, the azure sky and the lakes,
I cannot help but throw my bloated body into her bosom. Because I know
She never rejects those who she loves.

Did you know

It was here my fellows were imprisoned;
It was here the Defender of Faith Chushi Gangdruk was defeated.

It is here the smoke of the burning branches of mulberry trees swirl,
And the sound of spiral shell horns can be heard,
The roofs are flanked with coloured prayer flags;
It is here, the chest of the plateau, my home,
Tibet!

—Preface

0,

In the early morning I offer a bowl of purified water to Buddha,
I will no longer ask for more: the existence of Tibet,
Which has completed my life and repelled my fear of loss.

It is here I have encountered you
As well as all living things.
It is here I have experienced the feeling of love,
As well as the feeling of being loved.

Because I am a Tibetan,
I always firmly believe in history,
Always firmly believe
In the existence of sacred spirit.

1,

I hear different languages of different groups in my mother tongue, crying;
Those from blacksmiths, farmers, hunters,
From prostitutes, businessmen, vendors

I already disdain the scenes I'm seeing;
Although sometimes I still sing the Song of Emancipated Serfs,
I can recognise a guy with the sissy tone in his dialect must be a Shandong guy,
I can recognise a chick in the ugly photographer's vest is a Sichuan chick.

At this moment, I'm touching the damaged Buddha,
Wondering how it should be possible
That a month later all these people would gesture and speak in astonishment:
"Since Tibetans have religious beliefs, how can a Lama kill people?"
I think everything is dreadful for a reason.

Where else could we head for,
If the whole land is darkened by night?

2,

Because I'm a Tibetan, I have
A lot of memories:

The monkey and the demoness
With the nature of getting along with Mother Nature in harmony,
And, the Tibet Empire and the Tibetan song of Gesar orally passed from
generation to generation.

Because I'm a Tibetan,
I have been suffering from a life in misery;
Because I'm a Tibetan,
I have obtained enough comfort.

But it is in this autocratic winter
I composed this poem!

3,

"Her eyes and the wrinkles on her palms are Tibetan,
Her name, Tibetan,
Her dreams and sorrows, Tibetan,
Her belief, her legs and body, Tibetan,
Her language and her silence, Tibetan,
Her voice, Tibetan,
Her birth and death, Tibetan?"[1]

4,

How wonderful it is
To dream of parents!
I deeply believe that at this moment
I'm no longer in sorrow.

In this snowy night,
I get up to light a butter lamp.

I decide to take the prayer beads off my wrist
And pray to Buddha.

At this moment, the night seems so real and profound.

5,

Sky burial is
Not frightening at all,
In my eyes;
Benighted,
In your eyes.

Because I'm a Tibetan,
I understand myself.

6,

This time the rejection is
Related to your identity.
I said,
The Tibetan knife I carry with me every day is
Not for killing other lives.
You always wonder if in this world there ever exists a place

"Speak Tibetan because you are a Tibetan,
Celebrate Losar because you are a Tibetan."

In my mother tongue I answered,
Life and death are separated from each other.
I said I carry a knife with me
Because I soberly know who I am
And I want to intimidate myself.

7,

There they came on a Saturday afternoon.
There they came, in buses appearing as armoured cars.
There they came, with buzzing saws, ropes and other equipment.
There they came, the seven workers.
There they came, the seven devils.
There they came, holding beer bottles like flowers, drunk.
There they came, in camouflaged green outfits.

With bright red faces,
in black leather shoes,
There they came...[2]

8,

I am Tibetan,
I want to worship my gods in awe.
I am Tibetan,
I want to partake in all my religious festivals.
I am a Buddhist and I
Won't allow anyone to take away this
baptism of mine.

9,

How far must I go to arrive in the land of Tibet?
How far must I go to meet my parents?
How far must I go to wear Tibetan clothes?

Naked,
We are heading for Lhasa.
The festered feet as the proof,
That our bruised bodies and hearts are
Tibetan!

The garden is silent;
In the form of an eagle
Lhasa is flying.
Drawing near the thunder,
Comes soon the rain!

10,

Because we are Tibetan,
We are treated differently from other minorities:
Enduring aggravating discrimination, imprisonment, torture and death.
Because I am Tibetan,
I am no longer in fear of anything.
Still a courageous Buddhist,
I lit many lamps before our honoured Gods
In memory of my dead brethren
Just as usual.

Speaking in my mother tongue, I deeply believe that
At this moment, I feel peaceful and blessed!

Because I am Tibetan, I often ask
Apart from in Tibet, where else could we find a piece of land of the exiled
with such rich poetic sentiments?

10 February 2010

Notes:

1. An imitation of *A Lover from Palestine* by the Arabian poet Mahmoud Darwish

2. An excerpt from *Saturday Morning* by the Iraqi poet Yusuf

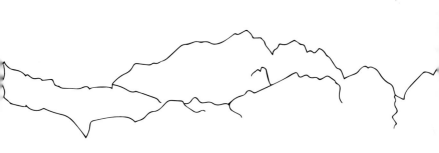

LHASA

ལྷ་ས།

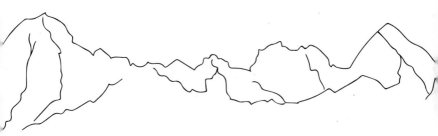

Woeser, 2013

EYE OF THE EMPIRE

Tsering Woeser

What kind of eye is that?
Yet, it must be an eye of utmost desires:
An eye of greed, anger, ignorance, jealousy, and pride - filled with wisps
of blood.
Among the Six Paths, this eye of all beings neither safe itself nor saved by,
And such is then accordant with the image of a powerful empire!
That day, he arrived without any invitation, the pale-faced scholar.
Keeping an overtly chastened smile
Yet his movements are not at all that modest,
As he quickly occupied the seat in the centre
Exposed his fangs like the glittering of frost and snow,
Revealed his claws like that of an eagle's sharp claws.
I dare not look into his eyes anymore,
His eyes are blazing with the five poisons
And it can easily control and capture souls.

Beijing
19 January 2018

Translated by Palden Gyal.

The poem very much relates to the image (shown opposite) of a surveillance
camera in Lhasa, presented in the guise of a prayer wheel.

Woeser, 2018

THE SPIDER OF YABZHI TAKTSER
Tsering Woeser

That afternoon the savage light
fell on ordinary, worldly faces,
the faces golden
as if stone were turned to gold,
transformed into unusual treasure.

We walked Jiangsu Road[1]. Yes,
the Jiangsu Road in the southern part of Lhasa.
The road's name is a violation that does not belong here—
    you understand?
Although I am older than my two friends,
I'm an *acha*[2] who's a full head shorter.
We spoke Tibetan, Chinese, and English,
although I only speak Chinese and Tibetan.
We were followed, I don't know by who or how many.
They were like tails we couldn't shake loose.
They stood there on the corners,
their eyes like cunning rats,
with their tiny swallowed hearts,
such trembling, wretched obsequious worms.
And there in the shadows of the roadside trees
people milled about outside of shops
their faces void of light
discussing business
riddled with anxiety.

We walked through Central Beijing Road[3],
this holy city so long ago embedded with foreign names.
Each name is like its own occupation—one after another,
everyone's grown so accustomed to them,
no one knows to think the names are strange.
Sunshine, ah, golden sunshine,
our warm shadows fell long across the colorful floor tiles.
Surveillance cameras everywhere[4]
hung in the high places
their eyes fell upon our bodies
on everyone's bodies—
    it seemed our backs grew cold.
Even so, I didn't want to turn my head to look.
I didn't want to stop,

I just wanted to keep going forward
and so we walked with long strides.
We grinned and laughed—
we were so handsome
cherishing this moment of apparent freedom
and together we sighed the slogan of the oppressor
    "So Happy and Blessed!"[5]

Go straight, then turn right—
how many times have I returned to visit *Yabzhi Takster*?[6]
This mansion which carries the family name of His Holiness[7]
was built more than sixty years ago, half of it already in ruins.
However, I don't want to retell history—
the earliest happy gathering,
the rapid tumble to impermanence
after being forced to abandon it,
the tears they shed while leaving.
Those who occupied it were outsiders
who wore green clothes, blue clothes,
outsiders reincarnated as hungry ghosts,
reincarnated as hermit crabs occupying the shell of another.
Today, the ancient orchards and gardens
have become a parking lot
a Sichuan restaurant
a shopping mall.
Many parts of the main building
and the outer courtyards have collapsed,
almost no windows still intact.

We stood on the roof of a nearby market
and looked down.
I was astonished at this huge wound that cannot be healed
astonished to see the mansion was so close to the *Phodrang Potala*[8]
    —so close, so close.

I harbored tears filled with self-criticism:
I'm an incapable, powerless waste.

We walked into the empty wilderness of the outer courtyard
half-filled with weeds and wildflowers,
half-filled with bicycles and motorcycles.
A senseless warehouse.
A man and woman who seemed like workers
passed by carrying plastic bags.
Four or five tall, lacquer-black Mastiffs[9]

were chained in a corner downstairs
their eyes of desperation.
They could only show their sharp teeth,
could only utter futile barks.
They belonged to the owner of a nearby Sichuan restaurant
who was waiting to sell them at a good price.
A few days later when we snuck in again
we ran into him as he came to feed them.
He assumed the posture of the owner
but his bluff to expel us had no effect.
He called a man wearing a security uniform—a Tibetan—
to rid the place of us.
But I asked him in Tibetan, "Who is the real owner of this place?"
My question rendered him helpless,
    na, na, unable to form a sentence.

Walking up the stairs from the garbage-strewn ground floor
we held our breath as we passed
through a winding corridor crosshatched with cracks.
A few rows of iron railings purchased from India
had bloomed rust but were still sturdy,
their consecutive patterns of sunlight and shadow
framing an unknowable maze like a foreign country.
We leaned on a railing and looked around.
The original white walls were mottled,
the black window frames had split apart,
the ends of the eaves were carved
with sacred animals, magic clouds, and lotus flowers.
Rotten wood strained
to support the structure of the mansion
and in a dark hall lined with ten or so columns
several shabby tables and chairs were scattered about,
discarded by the last people who left.
A few beams of light
fell obliquely from a clear story
through flying dust, flickering phantoms
as if they were monks wearing masks slowly performing *Cham*[10]
I noticed a window to the northwest
through this opening lined with blades of glass
I could perfectly see the *Phodrang Potala*
and it seemed like I was looking into the past,
and saw, within all the worry and grief
of the first years of the occupation,
the commitment of the Venerable Youth[11].

I turned from this only to be shocked again
by a broken mirror hanging from a pillar.
I hung there, reflected as a helpless Self
carrying an expression
of the desire to hide from the world.
I didn't dare get closer,
I was scared I might catch a glimpse of a singular shadow
fleeing in a panic in the middle of the night,
1959.
I was scared I might hear His Holiness
who has passed most of his life in foreign countries,
might hear him whisper:
　　"*Your home, your friends, your country—suddenly lost...*"[12]

Is it possible
I lived here in a previous life?
That I endured all the parting?
Is it possible
in the past I was in so much pain
I did not want to live,
yet exhausted my mind just to survive?
Unexpectedly there rose the desire to escape
but still I lingered in this room filled with vestigial traces:
the walls covered with old portraits of popular Hong Kong stars,
a front page of Tibet Daily from over twenty years ago
covering news of the 14th National Congress of the Chinese Communist Party,
a completely shredded print of the Potala Palace,
Chinese characters pasted to some of the doors
reading 'Blessing' and 'Great Prosperity in the New Year.'
Another door carried the Chinese word 'Office' written in red lacquer
and pasted to yet another door, a deathly pale seal:
　　Petition presented on January 5, 2005...
And a long-bearded Chinese door god,
his right hand holding a pagoda,
his left hand lifting an iron hammer.
In one nook there was a goat skull with a pair of empty eyes
its two burned horns curling out
as if in the past it were desperate for help.
In another nook, the original *arkar*[13] floor was gone
and from the cracks there grew small blades of grass
full of life.
In another spot, a chunk of wood the size of your hand—
which must have been a gorgeous column cap that fell long ago:
the paint still there

the carving still there.
It was the essence of this ancient house—
I quietly slipped it into my backpack.

A single piece of turquoise[14] hangs from my neck
it is my secret guide
that led me to the destiny of my next encounter:

    Dom![15]

Hanging outside a broken window
and floating dangerously in midair,
dom, a spider trapped in threads it spit out itself,
floated on a web so thin it could almost not be seen.
It had already become a mummy
looking into the abyss,
into a section of tragic collapse.
Was it the only dead bit of life here?
Was it the only existing guardian here?
Had it overestimated its own position?
Had it wanted to capture these invincible demons?

Hanging in front of my eyes, the spider was another mirror,
its lacquer-black carapace glimmering in the traitorous light.
Through some kind of struggle, it had become a metaphor.
I dared not touch it, afraid that in that instant
it might disappear.

I think back to those years.
This symbolic animal must not have been the only one of its kind,
and there must have been the host's house pets too—
there must have been cats and mice
and dogs, the special Lhasa Apso, running back and forth
from the Buddha hall to the living room and the bedrooms
perhaps peacefully falling asleep.
And surely a big dog too?
I mean a Mastiff from the grasslands.
He would have stayed in the yard with the gatekeeper,
stood at the entrance of the main gate—loyal, devoted, invincible.

Dom—this is how one says 'spider' in Tibetan
    the m soft, almost non-existent.

Domthag—this is how one says 'spider web'
    the m subtle as if it were being swallowed.[16]

Compared with other lifeforms
the spider's vitality is perhaps more tenacious:
it is easier for it to hide itself in another place and survive.
And yet it is also easier for the spider to die alone
in a violent, unnatural death that goes unreported.

This spider, "born like a fortress to imprison enemies,"[17]
wove the world into a lifetime of web,
bound by and to itself,
unable to extricate itself from its own threads—

just like us
and our unfathomable fate.

Beijing
31 July – 3 August 2017

Translated by Ian Boyden
San Juan Island
19 September 2017

Translator's note: This is a poem of extraordinary scale and complexity. I called on many of my friends to help me figure out how to render it into English. My deepest thanks to Rong Sun, Dechen Pemba, Jim Canary, Jennifer Boyden, and Sam Hamill for their insights and suggestions. And my great gratitude to Tsering Woeser for her patience with my many questions as I worked to understand the poem as completely as I possibly could.

Notes:

1. *Jiangsu Road*. Almost all the endnotes to this poem have to do with names and language, and how they constitute one of the primary means by which we form cultural identity. After the Chinese occupied Tibet in the 1950s, they quickly started to attack the Tibetan language. They renamed the streets, buildings, and cultural landmarks with Chinese names, even changing the names of mountains and rivers. Chinese was declared the state language, children were forced to attend Chinese schools, official documents were written in Chinese, and so forth. These foreign names are much more than symbolic, they are like weapons of the occupier, slowly erasing the cultural memory of Lhasa and Tibet as a whole. If you look at Tibet today on Google Maps, you will see this erasure in action, you will see a landscape of Chinese names. In the case of Jiangsu Road, Jiangsu is a province in eastern China, a part of historical Han China. Jiangsu has nothing to do with historical Tibet. The road was given this name on August 27 1997 in 'honor' of Jiangsu province funding the Chinese 'modernization' of this part of Lhasa. What was Jiangsu Road before it was Jiangsu Road? It was a road called Golden

Pearl Road built by the People's Liberation Army (PLA) shortly after they occupied the city in 1959. Before that, there was no road at all—it was a giant stretch of forested parks, foot paths, and little streams. When the PLA entered Lhasa they cut down this area and turned it into a military barracks, which was then linked by this new road.

2. *Acha* (ཨ་ཅག): Tibetan meaning 'older sister'. Tsering Woeser is originally from Lhasa and speaks both Tibetan and Chinese. However, she writes almost exclusively in Chinese. In this poem, she utilises many Tibetan words transliterated into Chinese, consciously choosing to not use existing Chinese words. She could have chosen the Chinese word for older sister, but her conscious choice of *acha* indicates that her relationship with her friends continues to be defined by Tibetan culture. The choice forces her Chinese readers to stumble into the unfamiliar. I have chosen to italicise these Tibetan words as they appear in the translation with footnotes showing the original word in Tibetan and their meaning. The transliterations are roughly based on the Wylie transliteration system, but have been modified to reflect how the words are pronounced in Lhasa, where Woeser is from and where the poem takes place.

3. *Central Beijing Road.* Like the name Jiangsu Road discussed in note 1, Beijing has nothing to do with historical Tibet. The original Tibetan name of Beijing Road was Dekyi Namgang (བདེ་སྐྱིད་གནས་གང་།), which means 'Happiness Road.' After the Chinese occupation, the road was expanded, cutting through numerous parks and wild lands to form the continuum of East Beijing Road, Central Beijing Road, and West Beijing Road, one of the main arteries of the city. In her essay *The New Face of Lhasa* Woeser writes, "Lhasa is submerged in a pile of new names that have nothing to do with its history, tradition, or culture. The outsider 'liberators' came and took over the old city of Tibet that had nothing to do with them, and have constructed a logic for reassigning revolutionary names that is unoriginal and completely domineering."

4. Today, Lhasa is covered in security cameras. They surround all of the major monuments and civic buildings. Chinese snipers are positioned on the top of many buildings, keeping watch for any individual or group protest that might break out. Han Chinese are more free to wander the streets of Lhasa than the native Tibetans.

5. Woeser told me that as she and her friends walked along the streets that day, they tried to imagine they were Han Chinese, but that everything became imbued with irony. "So Happy and Blessed!" is a common phrase used in Chinese propaganda regarding Tibet. Tibetans are presented as an idyllic people, "so happy and blessed," who were saved by Chinese liberation. In 2012, there was a large sculpture placed in the centre of Lhasa that reads "The Happy and Blessed City." It was meant to look like an abstract Tibetan style cloud, but the Tibetans laughed saying it looked like a giant pile of shit.

6. *Yabzhi Taktser* (ཡབ་གཞིས་སྟག་འཚེར་) is the family name of the 14th Dalai Lama. According to tradition this is also the name of this mansion. After the family of the Dalai Lama moved from Amdo to Lhasa, they built this mansion and gave it this name. It is located in the center of Lhasa, close to the Potala Palace. For more detail see Woeser's essay *The Ruins of Yabzhi Taktser.*

7. *His Holiness.* Tibetans have a multitude of names for the Dalai Lama including Yeshe Norbu, Gongsachog, Chenrezig, Gyalwa Rinpoche, and Kundun. In fact, most Tibetans usually do not refer to him by the name Dalai Lama. The reason

is that 'Dalai Lama,' meaning 'Ocean of Wisdom,' is actually a Mongolian name given to his lineage by the Mongolian King Altan Khan in the 16th century. 'Dalai' is a Mongolian word meaning 'Ocean' combined with the Tibetan word 'Lama' meaning 'Wisdom.' In this poem, Woeser refers to him as 尊者, meaning 'Venerable One,' and which corresponds to the English appellation 'His Holiness.' It is interesting to note that the terms 'His Holiness' and '尊者' are not translations of a specific Tibetan term, but are rather terms that originated within the Tibetan exile communities post 1959. As a major theme of this poem has to do with names and how they shape our consciousness, it is important to point out how Woeser refers to the most important spiritual leader of the Tibetan tradition.

8. *Phodrang Potala* (ཕོ་བྲང་པོ་ཏ་ལ་) is the Tibetan name for the Potala Palace. The Potala Palace is the most famous building in Tibet. It was the residence of the Dalai Lama until 1959 as well as the seat of the Tibetan government.

9. *Tibetan Mastiff, dokyi* (འདོགས་ཁྱི). In her essay *The Tibetan Mastiff as a Metaphor*, Woeser describes how in recent years the Tibetan Mastiff has become the favorite pet of Chinese tycoons. The thirst for these dogs has led to these dogs being stolen from Tibetans across the Tibet and sold at incredible prices in China. But then the market for these dogs collapsed and they were no longer cherished and were then sold to be eaten in hotpot restaurants. She sees this as a metaphor for the relationship of Han Chinese to Tibetans. The Han Chinese treat Tibetans in the same way they treat their pets.

10. *Cham* (འཆམ): A form of Tibetan religious dance performed by monks.

11. *Venerable Youth*, a reference to the young Dalai Lama.

12. This quotation is from *In Exile from the Land of Snows: The Definitive Account of the Dalai Lama and Tibet Since the Chinese Conquest* by John F. Avedon (Harper Perennial, 1997).

13. *Arkar* (ཨར་དཀར): Tibetan word meaning 'white material.' It is used in Tibetan buildings, made from weathered limestone or sandstone pounded into powder. It is generally used for the floors and roofs of buildings. During construction it is mixed with water, applied to the surface, and polished. After construction it is smooth, solid, and impermeable, like cement. There is a folk song: "*Arkar* is not a stone, *Arkar* is not the soil, *Arkar* is the essence of the essence of the lotus land from deep within the mountains."

14. *Turquoise, gyu* (གཡུ): Among Tibetan people turquoise is also known as a bla stone or 'soul stone.' Namkhai Norbu writes: "According to Tibetan tradition, the bla can have a support or be personified by an object, like a precious stone, a mountain, a lake, etc." (p. 225). Turquoise "is a *bla* stone to attract the oath-bound deities" (p. 5). Namkhai Norbu, *Drung, Deu and Bon: Narrations, Symbolic Languages and the Bon Tradition on Ancient Tibet*, translated from Tibetan into Italian, edited, and annotated by Adriano Clemente; translated from Italian into English by Andrew Lukianowicz (Dharamsala: Library of Tibetan Works and Archives, 1995).

15. *Dom* (སྡོམ): Tibetan, meaning 'spider.' Because Chinese is not written with an alphabet, it is very inhospitable to transliterating words from other languages. Foreign words are rendered using a combination of Chinese characters that approximate the

sounds, which invariably sound very awkward and a far cry from the original. And while the Chinese characters used are selected for sound, nevertheless, they also have their own Chinese meaning, which sometimes adds a new layer of potential meaning to the transliterated word. As there is no standard system for transliterating Tibetan words into Chinese, Woeser often makes them up herself, which means she has the chance of selecting Chinese characters not just for sound but also for meaning. *Dom* represents a delightful example. She originally chose the characters 董木, (*dōngmù*). At one point in our correspondence regarding the translation of this poem, I wrote, "I love that the word *dom*, as transliterated into English, contains the fundamental Sanskrit seed syllable *Om*—the cosmic, immutable sound, which forms a fundamental part of Buddhist chants such as *Om mani padme hūm*. Your entire poem is like a spider web revolving around this single word *dom*, it is the seed syllable of the poem. If I were to transliterate it into Chinese I would utilise the character 嗡, which means both *Om* and the buzzing of insects. Both predator and prey, a poem within the poem, like a secret sword." To my delight Woeser accepted this proposal and changed the transliteration to 特嗡母 (*tèwēngmu*), meaning 'mother of the extraordinary *Om*.'

16. *Domthag* (སྦྲ་ཐག): Tibetan, meaning 'spider web.'

17. This phrase is from the *Epic of King Gesar* in a passage about the extraordinary beauty of Gesar's stepbrother Gyatsa Shelkar, translated in Namkhai Norbu's *Drung, Deu and Bon* (p.5). By incorporating this quote, Woeser allies her poem with the *Epic of King Gesar* and the ancient Tibetan narratives known as *drung*, which record history, customs, and habits of the Tibetans and are often enriched with allegorical and poetic details. She said she was not forging a direct relationship between Shelkar and the spider, rather she wanted to invoke the beauty of the language in that passage.

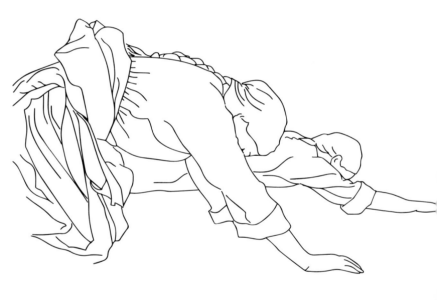

TODAY, I WISH TO OFFER THREE PROSTRATIONS TOWARDS LHASA

Theurang aka Tashi Rabten

My dinner last night was terror and anxiety
When the spies strolled the cafes and streets of Ngaba,
I dreamt of Lhasa dreaming of red blood dripping,
Green footprints appearing underneath the bloodied hands;
Waking up in the morning I remembered myself
I stroked my head with my right hand
My long hair is not cut,
I checked my feet with my left hand
They are not shackled.
This morning affection walks on street number 10,
Affection, the origin of our fathers and mothers,
The tsenpo Bod or the kingdom of Tibet
Too is affection,
In short that is who I am.
Food at the D restaurant tasted burned
Like the smouldering of my flesh and bones,
The smile of the waiter resembled an approaching red cliff
From which some guests are tumbling down
Some at the back are being thrown down;
Many chat in Tibetan on QQ
I don't know each of them by name
But I understand the language they write in,
This proves that we are of the same blood.
Can't people of same blood be in touch with each other?
It's not been long since I am holding this Apple,
I am a prisoner.
It's not been long since I've been out of that door,
My friends do not have much knowledge about this
But I think the spies have very good information on it.
I write poetry in the space meant for messages
Because I have so many things to tell,
Because I have joys, sorrows and resentments,
I have feelings that I cannot accommodate inside me.
You have asked me about many issues
I have responded to them honestly.
However,
I alone am the owner of these thoughts.
He who is imbued with power and authority
Is bound to tell others not to think too much,

Yet someone who respects freedom will never say 'YES'.
I am sorry,
Do you have any other questions?
Did I commit any crime?
Do I get punished for my answers?
If not, let me go.
I am feeling a little cold today,
And very terrified,
I want to get out and offer three prostrations towards Lhasa.

Translated by Bhuchung D. Sonam

Today, I Wish to Offer Three Prostrations towards Lhasa first appeared on social media around 19 March 2015 and the English translation has been kindly provided by exiled Tibetan poet Bhuchung D. Sonam.

WATERFALL OF BEER
Rinpung Tenchoe

The lush green field,
The fair and tender young woman,
The melodious and gentle song,
The bright covetous young man...

Ai ma!

But even more beautiful than these,
This expansive grove before us,
A mountain-like pile of beer.

Look!

The waves of foam jump to the sky,
The bar girl, a deceitful vixen,
A peacock's plumage, a bitch's tail,
The belly of a dzo,

Listen!

The sound of the bar girl's song is sweet and smooth,
That drinking song is the song of Tibet,
Chinese melody, Western narrative,
Indian tune,

Kye!

This is no ordinary beer...
To deceive the high officials, to be fearful of the Lamas!
The squandered wealth of the youth, the danger of the decline of old age.
The pain of losing a lover,
This is the youthful beer of all the youthful people of the Land of the Snows,
This is the joy of all the 21st century millennial Tibetans.
Mortgaging positions, provoking altercations, testimony to our youth.

Kye kye!

Beer of the waterfall, Waterfall of beer,
You own fearless marketplaces and unwavering clientele,
Endless consequences, undisturbed notifications,
Where did this guest who cannot get drunk come from?

Yes!

A pilgrim from outside of the three spring months,
A traveller who burst out from the earth of the three summer months,
The ingratiation shown by different work-units during the three autumn months,
The expenses of the celebrations of the three winter months,

Among others,

Lhasa, Budweiser, wheat beer, barley wine, in short the liquor of backdoor connections!
The liquor of accomplishment, the liquor of misfortune, the liquor of divorce,
Beer makes a man into a hundred and eight, liquor a man into a hundred thousand,

You are the courage-inducing tonic,
And so you open the door to violence,
You are an awareness-deluding tonic,
And so you dare to sleep with your best friend's wife,

You possess the proud spirit of appraising new customers,
Your vision is long reaching and your messages spread far and wide,
You separate those with low tolerance and those with sour taste,
While the expenditure amasses,
You cast off inhibitions, and endow all with the ability to converse and enrich civilisation with the imprints of all aspects of yourself.

Oh Beer!

You are witness to bribery and,
You are the step ladder to position,
You, in each undefiled drop of alcohol,
Record the waxing and waning of all farmers and nomads,
You, in each particle blown to smithereens –
Compile the rise and fall of all in civil service,

Without you,
How could I produce the love I show to my beautiful beloved!

Without you,
How could I satisfy the high and mighty officials?

Without you,
I wouldn't be able to shake a steady relationship?
How could I destroy the future of the children and the morals of society?

Maybe,
You are a vase made of a water crystal,
The filth in the rubbish, the vomit of a drunk,
The urine of a layabout, naturally occurring powdered ash,

But,

You possess the nature of attachment, and all those who love liquor the three times become your followers,
Forever bereft of awareness,
Reality is disturbing and you outline a hundred answers – how could it be worse than this?

The reason being,

Your benefits have fused with reality,
And your abilities having mixed with variegated actions,
Your many tangible benefits, have given many people profits and advantages,
Your real misfortunes, have plunged many people's lives and livelihoods into terror,

Did you hear? Oh Beer!

Did you hear the questions of a youth who has never tasted beer?
If the national economy falls into recession; what will you do?
If the harmonious familial relationship falls to pieces; what will you do?
If your children's futures turn to ashes; what will you do?
If your parent's eyes are seized by death; what will you do?

If your wife sleeps alone every night; what will you do?
If your gambling hands are empty; what will you do?

Oh yes, dear beer.

The chaos sewn by your hands, these reality-reflecting questions are etched into our hearts like rock carvings.
Really, you ability-inducing beer cannot be replaced by a cup of hot water.
How can the smell of trouble and a friend's profits replace health and longevity?
On the shoulders of this rarely attained human birth,
If, you don't possess an awareness accordant to the times
How can you ascend to pulsing vitality,
You will not be able stride forward!
A life of happiness even more unreachable!

Ko yi! Oh beer!

Your languidly overflowing froth,
These indiscriminately strewn bottles
Symbolise the drinking appetites of the new generation of the Land of the Snows,
These indiscriminately established bars and chaotic nangma bars,
You will meet the authentic thoughts of the new generation of the Land of the Snows,

Trouble, fighting, jealousy, hatred.
In this century we have no objects of engagement,
Lazy, backward and ill-behaved.
In this century we have no sacred places.

Beer, oh beer,

Our minds wax and wane with you, Our bodies deteriorate with you,
Even though the path ahead requires an exertion greater than before,
The youth of Tibet are without the necessary power of mind,
They hold beer to be the new path for our people,

Look, these ready drunks are the new generation of the Land of the Snows,
Listen, the sound of these backward footsteps are tread by the new generation of the Land of the Snows,

The dark nangma, shameless grandmothers,
Outwardly magnificent bars, jobless women,
The marketplace of beer is insuppressible,
The buyers of beer are relentless,

This pile of beer is from the pockets of the new generation of the Land of the
Snows,
This waterfall of beer is the product of the vigour of the new generation of the
Land of the Snows.

Translated by Yingsel

Waterfall of Beer was first posted on the blog TB Sheep on 7 March 2015.
Composed by blogger and poet Rinpung Tenchoe, the poem is a modern
adaptation of Dhondup Gyal's seminal 1984 poem *Waterfall of Youth* and
presents a satirical critique of contemporary Lhasa society.

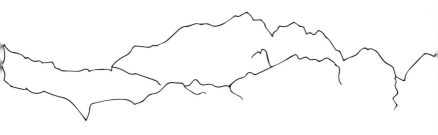

THE ENVIRONMENT

ཁོར་ཡུག

300 anti-mining protestors in Amdo, east Tibet. June 2016

THOSE PEOPLE

Theurang

Mountains hollowed out, rivers befouled
And wildlife wiped out.
Those people burrow our land
With their fangs and claws.

Pastures denuded, forests demolished
Boundaries of fields and pens dissolved and
Converted into extensive spaces of foreign, unhealthy trees.
Those guests have now settled, unapologetically.

Rangelands divided, fenced with iron enclosures
Livestock disturbed, and its population dwindling.
With fierce expressions, they snatch away slabs of our gold ores
And with unblushing smiles, they reward us with a few sacks of flour.
Those people really know how to ingratiate themselves.

Law. Policy. Harmony.

Those people have chains, locks
And awfully tight snares.

22 May 2016

Translated by Palden Gyal

This poem by Tashi Rabten, writing under his pen name, Theurang was written on 22 May 2016 and circulated on WeChat. In the poem, Theurang tackles the issue of mining in Tibet.

A WAY TO REMEMBER KHAWA NYINGCHAK
Gosher (Go Sherab Gyatso)

Since birth and death are inevitable, and the ultimate nature of phenomena as conditions of existence, of the billions of human beings on earth scattered across the continents like clusters of ant colonies, every day thousands and thousands meet their ultimate finality in different circumstances. Of the small crowd of my acquaintances, every now and then, regardless of age, I see people die and disappear like a streak of lightning. To be honest, quite naturally, I grieve and mourn each acquaintance's death differently. I think considerations like a person's efforts and exploits, the cause of his or her demise, and my own personal relationship with the individual chiefly influence how I mourn a death.

Last night, I heard of Khawa's sudden death. Personally, we were not close friends, and my acquaintance with him was limited to a few meetings and conversations. Nevertheless, the news of his sudden demise gave me an unusual sense of bereavement and heartache. The tragic news of his death haunted my whole day. Yes, it is true, as many would agree; Khawa was one of the most promising young Tibetan writers, and as a rare kind of intelligent and dedicated young Tibetan, it is indeed a tremendous loss. But, let's not talk about this or remember him this way. One might rebuke me if I continue, quite accurately perhaps, that, "It is characteristic of Tibetans to admire and elevate the dead and detest and loathe the living." Be that as it may, I think there is one significant issue that we cannot avoid thinking and remembering about Khawa. He was an individual who sacrificed his precious human life in order to protect the natural environment and the ecology of Tso-Ngonpo Lake.

These days we hear from both the government as well as individual experts that the ecological condition of the Tibetan plateau is extremely fragile yet it is so significant because the impact of its degradation affects not just Tibetans but billions of people across Asia. We hear this catchphrase of "environmental protection and conservation" almost like the mani mantra of our daily prayers. Despite all the mantras, I wonder why there are increasing number of cases of environmental destruction and ecological disturbance across the plateau. In the midst of all the mantras and sloganised promotions of "environmental protection and conservation," our mountains and grasslands, our lakes and rivers, and our wildlife and forests are increasingly "illegally" demolished, defaced and decimated. When the hearts, eyes, and all parts of Mother Nature are sheared off in different regions of the Tibetan plateau, where are our "environmental protection laws"? Where did the Offices of Nature and Environmental Protection go? Where did the police and security personnel run away to? No, they have not gone anywhere. When you observe it closely, it is the connivance of the local officials with wealthy businessmen engaged in the vicious activity of destroying the environment. As a result, even the most sacred lake of the Tibetan plateau (Tso-Ngonpo), the beautiful turquoise mirror smiling across the chest of the Plateau, is fraught with fishnets set "illegally" by greedy businessmen in collusion with local officials. The prevention of such illegal activities is not the responsibility of a writer who has nothing but a pen in his hand. It is the unavoidable responsibility of those Offices with elegant signboards hanging on their walls. Isn't it for that purpose and service we pay our taxes that feed and clothe them?

However, last night, when Tso-Ngonpo, the turquoise mirror of the Tibetan plateau, was annexed by an army of steel-fishnets and her gold fish panicked, those tax-funded officials must have gone to sleep, snoring and dreaming after satisfying themselves with alcoholic drinks and meaty dishes. There was no sign of them. Meanwhile, a young Tibetan who loved and adored his homeland sacrificed his life in an attempt to free the thousands and thousands of gold fish trapped in those nets. He dived deep into the sea, and left us forever. This young man was Khawa Nyingchak, a young Tibetan poet and author of children's stories, and who was also an environmental activist. His final act of conscience and sacrifice has made him a symbol of environmental protection and preservation. I hope we will remember Khawa Nangchak like the courageous Gyesang Sonam Dhargye who sacrificed his life protecting Tibetan antelopes in Achen Gang-gyab (dramatised in the 2004 film *Kekexili: Mountain Patrol*), and in his memory we should erect a statue of him visible prominently to the mountains, grasslands, lakes and gold fish of Tso-Ngonpo. In this way, we shall carry on Khawa's legacy and continue his dreams, and he can leave us in peace. It will inspire and serve as a wake-up call for Tibetans of this and future generations in raising awareness about protection and preservation of natural environment.

26 June 2015

Translated by Palden Gyal

The blogpost is by well-known Tibetan monk and intellectual Gosher (full name: Go Sherab Gyatso) and titled "A Way to Remember Khawa Nyingchak". It was written the day after Khawa Nyingchak's passing and posted on a Tibetan language website. In the post, Go Sherab Gyatso highlights important environmental concerns and issues for the area.

BEFORE LONG, PLANES WILL FLY IN MY HOMETOWN

My hometown is Amchok, the grassland on the southern bank of Sangchu River in South Gansu Prefecture. A few years earlier, people in my hometown were saying that in the near future there would be planes flying over our hometown. Since I heard these words, I have had pangs in my heart. But I haven't said anything about it as I thought it was just a rumour.

As months and years have flown by like a river, the rumour has become true and works have begun in my hometown before my eyes.

The news was announced in the Southern Gansu Newspaper. It was the year when I returned home just after I finished university. A notice was posted by a bank near my hometown, announcing the project had started. Finally this proved to me it was no longer a rumour.

The idle chatter has turned out to be true. The first step for planes to be able to fly over my hometown has commenced. During May 1, Labour Day holiday, I was back home. Some cadres, doctors, and some teachers arrived by car and visited every family with notices. They said that these papers were the official papers from the County government, and from tomorrow the project would be started. Also they said that some soldiers would guard the area and they warned us not to let the children play there. The people were asked to sign an acknowledgement and were given papers to sign.

Anyway, very soon planes will be flying over my hometown. Now there is another talking point in my hometown, people are saying: "After completing the airport project, our current homes will be destroyed completely and new buildings will be built because the current houses will be not be able to stand when the planes fly". These are the most reliable predictions of my hometown by people, based on what they know. In addition, building an airport could also be the first steps towards the building of a new city.

Evening of 1 June 2011

The blogpost is by a Tibetan blogger from Amdo who keeps a blog on the Tibetan-language blog-hosting site called "AmdoTibet". The blogpost was written on 1 June 2011 and posted online on 12 June 2011.

TO AMNYE MACHEN
The Plateau is my Home

Even though I have never seen you
Even though I have never been at your side
I know your stalwart figure
Standing firmly in the boundless space between heaven and earth

On your venerable forehead that has passed through thousands of years
Are the clean snowflakes shining in the sun of the plateau
Under your vast, peaceful and smooth feet
Is the sound of praises sung to you by the plateau herders.

You are one of the nine sacred mountains of Tibet
Your fame is firmly established throughout the world.
You are the Dharma defender of Amdo
Your good name is widely known.

However, today, the wheels of greed
Are running over the grassland, entering directly under your feet
They bring bombs, trucks, and excavators
And other bizarre tools that are used by demons
To excavate the hidden gems in your body

The people who have been guarding you for millions of years
Are unable to guard you anymore
They can only endure in silence
Their only choice is to wait helplessly…

One day they will be forced to move out
Saying goodbye tearfully to your beautiful and warm embrace.
Where will they go?
They will be placed on the edge of the barren desert

Henceforth, on our sacred Amnye Machen
The white flocks of sheep will never be seen again
The song of the herders will never be heard again
Those filthy greedy people will soon mercilessly stifle you

September 2011

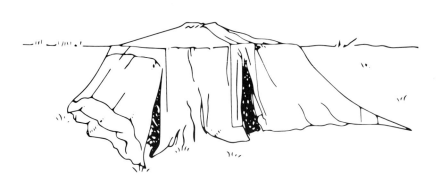

TONIGHT, I AM IN THE GRASSLANDS OF MY HOMETOWN
Shokjang

After heavy rainfall, I arrive at the grasslands of my hometown. Again, there is heavy rainfall, blocks of darkened clouds cover the grasslands of my hometown.

In the midst of this dense darkness, I am in a tin house. People call it a convenient house*. The convenient house was built this year. This is the first time I am staying in a convenient house.

The tin house is like the storied buildings in the city. There are a few doors and windows, I cannot see the darkness outside through the curtains. I cannot even see the tiny light penetrating through the cracks in the darkness.

Suddenly, I miss the black tent of the past, recalling the bright stars that can be seen from the opening on the top of the tent. The bursting pristine stars that can seen by everyone, remembering the scattering stars falling into my eyes as a star or two fell through the opening on the top of the tent. I remember reciting Mani, as though a life was extinguished each time a meteor fell through space.

Now, I have arrived in my hometown on the grasslands, the place I am staying in is the tin house. From the tin house I cannot see the stars. Stars that had fallen into my eyes in the past, now shatter into the vast space.

2 July 2014

Translated by Dhonling Bhu

* In Tibetan the word used is *tab de*, meaning convenient, which may be the modern usage of the word for the Chinese government policy known as "Comfortable Housing", more widely known as the resettlement of Tibetan nomads.

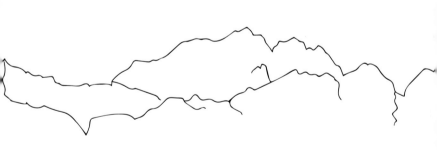

CONTEMPORARY TIBETAN ART AND ARTISTS

དེང་རབས་བོད་ཀྱི་སྒྱུ་རྩལ།

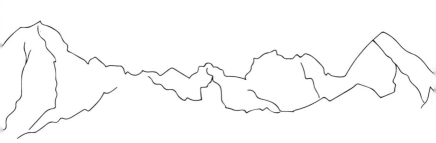

Scene in the Desert, 2014, photograph

INTERVIEW WITH NORTSE

Melong Art WeChat channel visits The Scorching Sun Art Lab and meets its founder Nortse on Lhasa River's Xianzu Island

'Art has the ability to present anxiety, confusion and suffering in a light way, without immediately terrifying the audience; art has the ability to slowly guide the audience to the spiritual core of a piece. This is my art.'

- Nortse

How would I describe my feeling of initially meeting Nortse?

Just like the uncle from next door, he made some delicious sweet tea, spoke standard Lhasa dialect and referred to me in honourific terms even though I am from a younger generation. Every now and then he would laugh somewhat bashfully and considerately pour me another cup of tea, patiently answering my, what I now feel were, rather naive and childish questions.

Others used to jokingly call Nortse "Lhasa's kindest artist", he is simply such a likeable person.

But when you face his artwork, you sense that the creator feels a scorching pain deep inside, you sense his cries for hope and also his silent contemplation. This was how I first felt when I encountered Nortse's piece titled *Scene in the Desert II*.

The depicted scene shows a vast barren desert that stretches along into the distance. The wind blows down from the snowy mountain and from the desert. The ancient Buddhist robes tower in the background, turning their backs to this world. We don't know if there is any flesh and bone wrapped up inside them. One just feels and hears the dry sand in one's mouth, the dry lips chanting prayers which are immediately swept away by the wild desert wind. A deep pain starts spreading from the pit of one's stomach.

Buddhist Robes

After meeting Nortse, the first thing I inquired about was the motivation behind and process of creating the piece *Scene in the Desert II*.

"I pay particular attention to Tibetan culture and religion every day and have always wanted to create something related to my own understandings about these issues. The Buddhist doctrine has been around for over 3000 years, but it has experienced a decline in today's society."

"In many monasteries, many monks would put up their robes after completing religious assemblies. So even after the bodies are gone, the robes still maintain their original shape and remain in their original space. When the robes come into contact with the desert and mix with this particular landscape, it creates a special kind of scenery.

"There is heavy wind in the desert and perhaps the robes will be blown away. This momentary feeling makes you full of sorrow. It seems as if one's own culture is becoming increasingly distanced from one's own body. Today, social change is massive, many people's only meaning in life is money, power and other external things. The lack of culture really makes us sad. The idea behind *Scene in the Desert II* is very simple, I don't think there are any deeper or more metaphorical meanings to be found in this piece."

"The background of *Scene in the Desert II* comes from an area near the airport on the way to Samye Monastery. There is a large patch of desert with a river next to it. That's where I created the piece. The robes I collected from several monasteries, some of them have a history of more than 200 years. Most of their original owners have already passed away and so they are used by the disciples. When they heard that I wanted to create this artwork, they just asked for a small symbolic amount of money and then gave the robes to me."

Scene in the Desert II, 2014, photograph

Self-Portrait

Apart from works revolving around ancient Buddhist robes, self-portraits are another important element of the artist.

Last year Hong Kong's Rossi & Rossi art gallery held an exhibition titled *Paper Dreams*; it included the self-portrait *Red Tablecloth I*.

Red Tablecloth, 2015, mixed media

The purpose of self-portraits is mainly for the artist to investigate the relationship between himself and his surrounding environment. Almost all of the men portrayed on the paintings are covered in masks or bandages. This is related to the experiences of the artist himself. His father was once injured and bed-ridden from a traffic accident; the self-portraits also include the many subtle feelings that the artist has accumulated and that all erupt at once.

"This is not a conscious effort, these are just feelings accumulated through the portrayal of what's in the heart."

Father's Violin, 2008, mixed media (digital photo, oil, acrylic) on cotton canvas

Dreams in Paper Boats, 2015, mixed media

Paper Boat

Another motif that reemerges in Nortse's paintings is the paper boat.

"Paper boats used to be the main toy for people from our generation when we were young. When the paper boat is placed into the stream, it carries along one's manifold beautiful visions of the future and it contains one's most remote aspirations; but it even more symbolises the sincerity and genuineness of little children."

The Models Dyed to Red, 2015, mixed media

"When I combine the image of the paper boat with the prayers of my own culture, all kinds of fantastic demons and alien patterns emerge in the Age of Dharma Decline of the sutras. 'When the iron bird flies in the sky, when the iron fish swims in the river, this is the time when dharma perishes.' What I want to portray are my innermost worries and anxieties."

Porcelain

Nortse also makes extensive use of ready-made materials to portray cultural change, industrialisation and the massive production of consumer goods. His most recent focus rests on cheap plastic imitations of porcelain tableware. These works are not as gentle and moderate as the Buddhist robes or the paper boats, they are made from randomly-patterned porcelain cuts, which he rearranged and reassembled into different shapes, creating a sharp and unconventional feeling.

Every time I create a new artwork, I hope that I can also open up a new, not walked-upon path. This is why I often look for new and different kinds of media and materials.

"This cheap porcelain is of extremely inferior quality and differs very little from the cheap disposable products sold at Lhasa's markets; but they look quite nice from the outside and are widely used by people on the grasslands and also by ordinary restaurants. Most of them are produced in small, illegal factories and they have a detrimental impacts on people's health; so the reason why I use them as media for my artworks is to draw attention to them; but the series is not mature yet, I am still at the exploratory stage."

By using these small, often overlooked items purchased at Lhasa's markets, the artist hopes to make us aware of how mass production as a characteristic of consumer culture is actually harming our bodies and our health. Additionally, processing these inferior materials also reflects how these mass-produced goods actually result in overall cultural damage.

Mandala II, 2015, mixed media

Finally, my discussion with Nortse returned to the topic of Tibetan contemporary art and its difficult situation.

"Tibetan contemporary art faces many major challenges. It is mainly a question of the environment. Contemporary art has no stable foundation in Tibet, not many people are practicing it, there are not many exhibitions, lectures or other events. The Gedun Choephel Artists Guild to which I belong has existed for over ten years; its original aim was to propagate and implement contemporary art in Tibet and its initial achievements were remarkable. But later, its development was impeded because of financial and other problems.

"The Scorching Sun Art Lab that I am currently developing used to be my own studio; artist Gade and I decided to create this space because we had encountered so many difficulties in organising exhibitions, so we now offer this place particularly for experimental and contemporary art.

The Scorching Sun Art Lab, photograph by Padma

"The Scorching Sun Art Lab has the purpose of creating a platform for artists from China and abroad to communicate with each other. We spare no efforts to promote and develop Tibetan contemporary art and even though, our influence is still very weak and we are not really understood by the majority of local audiences, I believe that the simple fact that we exist is already very valuable. Time will tell."

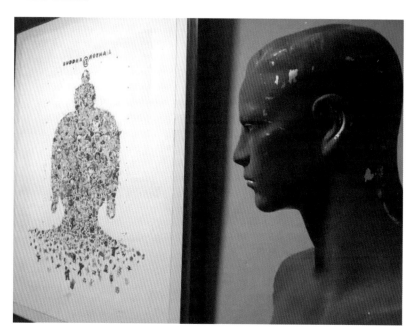

On the left Buddha@Hotmail, a work by artist Gongkar Gyatso; on the right an original object that Nortse uses for his paper artworks. Photo by Li Yu

So, Lhasa's most pioneering, most interesting and most impressive art space is slowly developing along Lhasa's riverside. In June 2016 a series of exhibitions and events will be launched here.

In the past, I participated in an exchange by Tibetan university students in Beijing and used my spare time to share some contemporary Tibetan art pieces. This might well inspire more people to inquire and learn about this form of art. Now, The Scorching Sun Art Lab provides even more vivid and professional commentary and explanations on contemporary Tibetan art.

A more beautiful era is approaching.

In the future, we will be able to enjoy higher quality exhibitions and more interesting lectures and screenings.

With Nortse as the representative, contemporary Tibetan art is currently establishing a relationship with Tibetan society and local culture.

Art provides a perspective to look at and understand the world; contemporary Tibetan art offers an alternative to the traditional and religious worldview: how should people like us of this day and age look at the world that we live in?

Since this interview and its launch in 2016, the Scorching Sun Lab has continued to hold regular exhibitions and events in Lhasa.

The ground floor of the gallery. Photo by Li Yu

A projector installation on the first floor. Photo by Li Yu

Little Red Book series No. 22, 2015

A BROKEN FLOWER BLOSSOMING IN THE CRACKS: TIBETAN ARTIST GADE TALKS ABOUT CONTEMPORARY TIBETAN ART

Tsesung Lhamo of Sweet Tea House WeChat channel

26 July 2016

First, I would like to know a bit about yourself; how did you get involved with art?

I liked drawing and painting from a very young age; I always thought I would become a painter, my goal has always been very clear and I was lucky that at every stage of my career I happened to meet a good teacher. I forgot who said this, but "a person who manages to do what he or she dreamt of doing as a child is a happy person". I feel that I am really happy, I have always been doing what I like. I have three teachers who I need to thank: Mr. Han Shuli, Mr. Yu Xiaodong and Mr. Li Xianting. They gave me the most important and most effective guidance during crucial periods of my artistic life. When I look back at my past works, I feel ashamed to have to say that I was once their student.

As one of the representatives of contemporary Tibetan art how do you define "contemporary art"?

I only represent myself (laughs). Contemporary art is "truth"! The definition of contemporary art is not really related to time; in other words, we cannot say that any art that is produced in the present is automatically contemporary art. It is first and foremost an artistic approach and cultural standpoint. Genuinely confronting one's own immediate experiences, feelings and living environment is the most important approach of contemporary artists. You need to express the things and events that you yourself have encountered, you have to express the real situation. In the past, we would never paint our own life experiences, because that would be too subjective. For instance Tibet, what is Tibet? Everyone has different ideas and different experiences and it is precisely these different elements that make up Tibet; it is not simply "the white clouds in the blue sky", "the snow mountain and the grasslands" or the "beautiful Buddhist temples". People from our generation are highly detached from our culture and mother tongue. After having been cut off from our spoken and written language as well as from our culture and history, can we really say that we represent Tibet? Early on, I would also paint a mystified Tibet, would contribute to the "Shangri-La-isation" of Tibet, would essentialise Tibet, but then I gradually came to think that this was fake. "Othering" Tibet is bad, but even worse is when Tibetans themselves "other" Tibet. Our own pieces of art are completely unrelated to your and my lives. This is why contemporary art has given me a voice; it is a tool that I can use to get as close to the truth as possible.

But there are still traditional elements in the techniques adopted by contemporary artists, right?

Yes, in my case this has always been true. I have always tried to bring traditional Tibetan art into a contemporary art context; I am still deeply fascinated by traditional Tibetan art. The attention to detail used in the techniques and the ability to create narratives is still very enchanting. These elements are not so important in western or Chinese art and I really want to continue this complex art of storytelling because it helps to express my intentions. It originated from an ancient language system, the so-called "native language system" of Tibetan art, which still exudes great vitality, only that it was broken off and has never been fully revived. The art history of any culture tells us that the evolution of art always begins and develops from one's very own cultural root. This is why contemporary Tibetan art must by no means become a recreation of western contemporary art. It has its very own language and value system.

In 2003, you collaborated with a few other local artists and initiated The Gedun Choephel Artists' Guild, how did you come up with this name? How was Lhasa's artistic atmosphere at the time and how did society look at contemporary art?

Gedun Choephel was a very cool person, it is hard to believe that during these times that such an unconventional Tibetan could exist. Many of his ideas would be regarded as revolutionary and avant-garde even today. I would regard him as the pioneer of Tibetan artistic and cultural enlightenment. For us, he is a symbol, a spiritual guide. His name is just so suitable for us.

The artistic atmosphere in Lhasa was still quite good back then. It wasn't so commercial yet. Everyone was young and passionate, we would often get together and fool around, it was a good artistic spirit. The level of acceptance in society was also quite good. There was no WeChat yet, you know, haha… not many people knew about us, most people who came to exhibitions were from our close circles, they knew what to expect. Today, on the other hand, it is really a little bit frightening how everything is disseminated via WeChat and Weibo; everyone knows everything and it is easy to become extremely popular. But today, there are also so many opinions and voices, even attacks and abuse from fellow Tibetans. I never experienced this in the past, but I have got used to it. We will even get attacked for eating KFC, won't we?!

Making Gods, 2011: "I would really like to know what a thangka without religious meaning looks like. On the other hand, in this era of globalisation, the deities that are of real use are not those in the temples, but those brought to us by the mainstream culture of globalisation; there are all kinds of 'outside deities', which is why I used various global cultural symbols to create this new deity."

Can we regard today's Scorching Sun Art Lab as the continuation of Gedun Choephel Artists' Guild? What has been continued and what is new?

Yes, we could call it a continuation. Gedun Choephel has been around for 13 years, but it has always been a somewhat loose group. The ideas of some of the members have also come to differ over time and when there are too many conflicting opinions, it becomes difficult to do anything. This is why Nortse wanted to independently run an art space to realise some of his own ideas without having to consult with everyone else first. He wanted me to support him which is why the two of us started The Scorching Sun Art Lab. But of course both of us will also always be members of Gedun Choephel. In fact, the first exhibition that we organised at Scorching Sun was The Gedun Choephel Artists' Guild 13th anniversary exhibition.

Scorching Sun is not only a platform for contemporary Tibetan art, we are hoping to express a more diverse range of ideas through it. We also hope that Scorching Sun will not become too big and commercial. Gedun Choephel hosts many professional artists, and the market forces us to make compromises. Scorching Sun is small and has little expenditure, it is located in our own place and so we don't have the pressure of paying rent, which is why we can just do whatever we want to do. It gives us more freedom. When Nortse and I want to do something, we do it and if it goes wrong, we don't impact other members. Scorching Sun doesn't only provide a space for members to exhibit their works, it is also open to young artists; we accept all good pieces, provide a space and help them become popular.

Our motto is to maintain a high standard, even if that means that we only have one exhibition per year. If the standard is too low, we would rather not do it. And there is no loss if we simply keep our doors shut. So, this space gives us an opportunity to exhibit more outstanding, experimental and forward-looking pieces of art. At the same time, we also hope to get Chinese or even international artists to give lectures, stay and paint or exhibit their works here. It is an opportunity to promote communication between different contemporary artists. For this, we secured the full support from Liao Wen. Owing to her help, we have already managed to cooperate with 10 Chinese contemporary art organisations and are gradually promoting further communication and cooperation between Tibetan and Chinese artists. But at this point, we are still at the trial stage. At this point, the entire project over here is supported and financed by Nortse and myself. Both of us like it, which is why we do it. I always say, when you have no expectations, you will not be disappointed. We have never applied to any foundations for extra funds. It has always just been the two of us. It is difficult to say how long we can keep doing it. I just hope that we can do it as long as possible.

Have you ever thought about charging for exhibitions or asking for financial help from external sources?

All our exhibitions are free for the general public. We have thought about asking for external financial help to continue to operate this space, but we don't have any commercial motives. What we are worried about is that if we do take money from other people, we will restrict ourselves and compromise our degree of freedom. This is why we are extremely cautious when it comes to seeking external financial help.

Where does the name Scorching Sun come from?

Scorching Sun is the transliteration of the Tibetan word ཉི་བཀྲག (*nyi bkrag* meaning "scorching sun"). Nortse came up with it. Originally, I suggested to simply call us Scorching Sun because our previous exhibition *Scorching Sun of Tibet* was very successful, it left a deep impression on many people in China, I thought it would be good to continue using this name. But Nortse wanted it to have more of a "Tibetan flavour", so we used "*nian zhe*" (念者), which is the Chinese transliteration of the Tibetan. But the two characters have no specific meaning.

The New Scripture: A recipe for hui guo rou, 2005

The New Scripture: An end of year resumé of van Gogh, 2005

2016 marks the 13th anniversary of Gedun Choephel Artists' Guild and simultaneously the birth of Scorching Sun Art Lab. Your first exhibition in the latter followed the theme *Journey from the Heart*, why did you pick this theme?

As I just said, I hope that the pieces exhibited in this space will express the innermost truths and ideas, starting from the heart; we don't want anything fake. In fact, regardless of whether it's Scorching Sun Art Lab or Gedun Choephel, the principle of contemporary art must be truth! Over the past 13 years we always fantasised as to what art could change, but eventually the truth always pulled us back into reality. Subsequently, we would always regress, regress and regress even more. Even though we worked hard, we worked in the wrong direction. On a different level, the theme had a second meaning, namely that of a new beginning, a new direction.

Speaking of Tibetan paintings, they often give people the impression that they are just *thangka* and murals in monasteries, but you and other contemporary artists use modern techniques to convey traditional culture whilst also reflecting contemporary society. In a sense you fill a gap in Tibetan art by expressing yourself and adding a modern component. So I would be interested in hearing what you have to say about the current state of contemporary Tibetan art and also its future.

The current situation is not very ideal. Firstly, the general environment is not good and secondly, the contemporary art market is crumbling, it is nowhere near as good as before 2008, when it was flourishing. Many people are simply making a run for it, trying to throw themselves into other artistic domains that have more promising markets; and we cannot blame them. But from a different perspective, all this is also positive, because it makes the opportunists retreat, leaving behind those who really like and care about this profession; it is a cleansing process, which isn't bad. As for the future, I am really not able to make any predictions.

I heard that you signed a contract with the famous art gallery Rossi & Rossi that collects art from the Himalayas. Can you tell us a bit more about your relationship with them?

Rossi & Rossi is a British art collector and dealer specialising in traditional Tibetan Buddhist art. I was introduced to Fabio Rossi by my American friend Ian. The first piece of contemporary art that he bought was my work. Subsequently, he provided some space to promote contemporary Tibetan art. We have been cooperating for over 10 years, opening up an international market for contemporary Tibetan art. Rossi & Rossi are the nationally and internationally leading gallery in systematically promoting contemporary Tibetan art. Two years ago, they set up a gallery in Hong Kong. Thanks to Rossi, I no longer need to worry about making a living from painting.

A Million Questions, 2011, installation

There are really only a few number of famous artists, most actually remain unknown and can never realise their dream during their lifetime. Vincent van Gogh, for instance, suffered when he was alive, but became huge after his death. What are your views on the relationship between art and business?

One cannot expect to immediately make money from painting. But one shouldn't think that artists have to live a life in deprivation either. Good artists will always be recognised by the market and have a certain value. I don't think art and business are contradicting each other. There are some artists out there who feel particularly virtuous and avoid any contact with the market, while others try to aggressively pursue commercial benefits. I think both extremes are bad. Artists accept your value judgement. That is normal. For example, if Michelangelo had not been supported by the Medici family, mankind's art history would be missing some extraordinarily amazing art works. We cannot always use van Gogh as proof that artists should regard money as dirty, have to be unhappy and cut off their ears!

You are exhibiting your work in Tibet, China and abroad. As an artist, which place do you like the most?

I have only been to very few places and at the moment I cannot go anywhere. So I don't have many choices. Luckily I had the chance to go to Nepal many years ago, so I like Nepal. The old streets and old temples made me feel at home and I would like to live there permanently.

What about Lhasa, how would you rate Lhasa's cultural life?

Does Lhasa have any cultural life? (laughs) I have not been to nightclub in I don't know how many years (laughs), I have no idea about Lhasa's culture and art scene.

This is part of it, no?

Haha… We hope it is, but it isn't much use. No matter how good the exhibition is, people look at it and forget about it again. No matter how big the event, people only remember it for about a week. How memorable can an art exhibition really be?

Out of all the exhibitions that you have organised, which one has left the deepest impression on you?

It would definitely be *Scorching Sun of Tibet* in 2010. It was planned by one of China's greatest contemporary artists Mr. Li Xianting. His academic status goes without saying and it was very important that someone like him, who assumes a formal and mainstream viewpoint, took an interest in contemporary Tibetan art. This exhibition was fundamentally different from previous Tibet-themed exhibitions in terms of its perspective and appearance. The world has always either admired or overlooked Tibetan art, but no one has ever approached it on an equal footing, it was never considered part of any artistic mainstream, but has always been marginalised, labelled as ethnic culture and regarded as exotic. I feel that this represents an unequal cultural attitude. So the fact that *Scorching Sun of Tibet* allowed them to look at and study our work on an equal footing has been very important in the history of Chinese contemporary art.

Ice Buddha, 2016

In 2006, you placed a statue of Buddha made from ice into Lhasa river and used photos to document how it slowly melted away. More recently, you reconstructed the ice statue at the foot of Mt. Kailash, at the lakeside of Mapam Yutso. Where did you get the inspiration for this ice Buddha? And why did you reconstruct it in Ngari?

I have talked about this ice Buddha too much, people even call me the "ice Buddha artist" (laughs). So in art you really cannot surpass yourself. If you happen to produce something very good and want to then produce something even better it is almost impossible. Always having to live in one's own shadow can be really painful. The idea behind this ice Buddha was to express the Buddhist notion of reincarnation. From nothing to something and then back to nothing; water turns into ice and ice slowly turns back into water; this is a kind of reincarnation. In the process of melting, the shape is constantly changing, it is a status of impermanence. But of course, there are many other interpretations of this piece. The artist is merely the creator, but the interpretation is left to the audience. The artist does not have the sole authority over the interpretation of his work.

I thought the piece represented global warming.

Yes, it can be interpreted as being about environmental protection, this is the nature of art works. Different people see different things: There are a thousand hamlets in a thousand people's eyes. And the ice Buddha is really open to interpretation. As to why I reconstructed it, well, originally I should have used video recording to capture the melting process, but didn't have the technology at the time. Plus, I suffer from extreme procrastination, never got round to doing it again. Ten years just passed in an instant. It's frightening when you think about it. Another reason is that I have always wanted to place an ice Buddha at every important river and holy lake in Tibet. So I decided to place one at the lakeside of Lake Mapam Yutso.

Finally, I would like to know which one would be the piece that you are most satisfied with, which piece was most difficult to produce and which one was the easiest?

During every stage of my artistic career, there are different pieces of different styles that I am most satisfied with. Early on in 1997 there was *Spirit Beings on a Yak Hide Raft* in memory of my mother. I was really happy with that painting and have kept it all along, have never wanted to sell it. Then there is the *New Scriptures Series* from 2010, a collection of 108 pieces, which should actually be called *Fake Scriptures*. I used traditional drawing techniques for all of them but completely changed the content of the scriptures, including text messages, popular stories etc. From far away it looks like an antiquity, but from close-up it becomes completely new; this is what Tibet feels like, many people's first

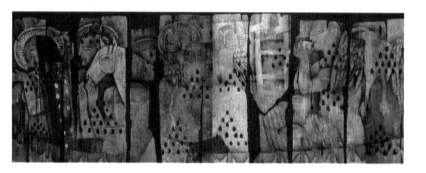

Spirit Beings on a Yak Hide Raft, 1997

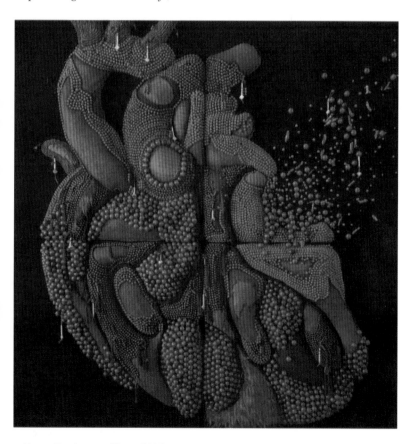

Prayer Beads series: Heart, 2015

impression is that of old, mysterious symbols, but once you live here, you will realise that it has totally changed and isn't so different from the rest of China.

The *Ice Buddha* is another piece that I am quite happy with. Later on, the series of installations called *Making Gods*, including *The Prayer Wheel*, *The White Book* or *The Black Scriptures* ... the more recent *Prayer Beads* series is another one. I used prayer beads to make a heart and a sun; I find prayer beads interesting as a medium. They are full of people's prayers and hopes, when you take up prayer beads, it is like immediately communicating with Buddha; similar to the mobile phone today, when you don't have it you feel like being on an isolated island; when you hold prayer beads, you feel safe. This is why I decided to do something with them, I feel they have a profound meaning. In fact, I started working with them three years ago and have produced almost 20 items, but I am only really happy with three or four of them.

The most difficult piece was a series of paintings that I did two years ago; I spent six months painting 12 hours per day until I started vomiting blood. I used many different techniques used for *thangkas*. It was really distressing for my eyes. I came to realise how difficult the life of *thangka* masters must be, so next time you go and buy a *thangka*, don't even think about bargaining (laughs). Recently, I try to paint smaller pieces, I don't want to get myself into trouble anymore, you know I am getting old… (laughs). Finally, the *Bodhi Leaves* series has been quite relaxing; I could finish one per day. When I had an idea I would paint, otherwise I would just leave it. But it's important that it isn't so demanding. I am planning to eventually complete a series of 108 bodhi leaves.

Ok, this is the end of the interview, thank you so much for your time. I was really happy to talk to you about contemporary Tibetan art and I really hope that more people will follow your group and contemporary Tibetan art.

I thank Sweet Tea House and you for this interview.

HER PART ONE: TIBETAN FEMALE ART EXHIBITION SERIES
Gade

17 September 2017

Jomo Lhazom Cultural Group, Tibetan Women's Platform and The Scorching Sun Art Lab jointly launch *HER*, a series of exhibitions in Lhasa showing the works of outstanding Tibetan female artists in different artistic realms, including fine arts, literature, music, film, dance and fashion.

During each exhibition, one artistic category will be chosen and displayed. In this way, we can do justice to each female artist and systematically prepare their works; also, each exhibition can thus be more thorough and profound. We really hope that this series can establish itself and continue and that female artists in various artistic realms, including their personal information, can be turned into and published in the form of a collective works. Plus, this is also a great opportunity to compile an archive and document contemporary female artists in Tibet for the future.

In *HER* Part One, five female artists are exhibited: Tsering Dolma, Dangsel Dawa, Tsering Lhamo, Dedron, Nyedron.

I remember how over ten years ago, we once curated an exhibition on female artists in cooperation with The Gedun Choephel Artists Guild. The exhibiting artists were, of course, identical with the names above, apart from Nyedron. Even though over ten years have passed since, the name list has not changed much. Trying to find a new female face among Tibetan artists is really very tough. I believe that this situation should be one of the problems that this exhibition reflects upon. Luckily the above female artists have never given up producing art; so now we are able to launch this exhibition.

TSERING DOLMA

Born in 1966 in Lhasa; graduated in fine arts from the Department of Art of the University of Tibet; fine arts teacher at the Lhasa High School, Lhasa Normal Polytechnic; member of the Chinese Artist Association; vice-chairperson of the Lhasa China Federation of Literary and Arts Association (CFLAC); her work New Painting Show *was selected for the 6th National Art Exhibition;* Reincarnation *was nominated for the Minority Hundred Flowers award and entered into the 4th China Minority Art Exhibition; many of her works have been collected by different art organisations and collectors around the world.*

Her paintings always remind me of the traditional "*Lama Mani*" (it is a kind of folk art that involves drawings and words). Especially the technique she uses to portray characters in her paintings has much resemblance with folk art.

Her works are not as exquisite as *thangka* paintings, in some cases even showing some slightly coarse strokes; they are simple and direct; but they are also piercingly smart, which is quite different from the characteristics usually attributed to female art works.

Her works are permeated with narratives, for example, her series titled *Birth, Age, Sickness, Death* as well as the *Returning from the Grave* series that is shown at this exhibition. Narratives are generally excluded in western contemporary art and also in the Chinese painting system. But this is precisely the native language system of Tibetan art.

What is the distinctive form of narration of contemporary Tibetan art? This is a question that I have always been thinking about. I believe that the art of each region has to be rooted in its own context and cultural environment. Perhaps, we have been brainwashed by the thoughts of western modernism, our perspectives and ways of expression have been particularly drilled, perhaps we have long forgotten how to speak and express ourselves.

But Tsering Dolma has mastered this native way of expression, integrating it in her very personal experience. On the surface she seems to use paintings to depict the suffering of human life as narrated in Buddhist scriptures, but you will slowly realise that every single stroke tells Tsering Dolma's very own story, narrating each period of her very own life.

Left: Tsering Dolma
Right: A painting from the *Returning from the Grave* series

LANGDUN DEDRON

Born in 1976 in Lhasa; graduated in fine arts from the Department of Art of the University of Tibet; in 2009, she held her own art exhibition at Rossi & Rossi in London titled Nearest to the Sun; *in 2011, she was honoured with the title "China Art Weekly Person of the Year;" in 2013 she became vice-chairperson of the Tibet Art Association and a member of the China Art Association; in Italy, she held the* Dedron *exhibition; her works have been collected by the Likeran Arts Foundation, by art galleries in the UK and the US, museums and private collectors.*

Looking at her works is a relaxing and happy experience. This is also her artistic vision, she wants people to enjoy her art. In the same way as Tsering Dolma, her works have their roots in traditional Tibetan art. As a student she indulged in models and colours of ancient Tibetan drawings; but she did not simply copy them, she also always added her own innovations, techniques and ways of expression, which led to the formation of her very own, unique artistic language.

Above: Langdun Dedron
Left: From my Grandparents to my Son

Regardless of whether she depicts people, birds, flowers, fish or insects, her works are full of the spirituality and qualities of the plateau. I regard Dedron's way of looking at things as particularly important, a very sharp and keen quality, it is a natural gift, which is very difficult to acquire through study. So all the life that she creates with her brush is full of spirituality. This is also a typical Tibetan way of expression, which is deeply rooted in the Tibetan artistic language system. Dedron managed to activate this system using her very own modes of artistic expression.

Over the past few years, Dedron's works have shifted from depicting the bold and imaginative mysterious garden to her personal life, like *From my Grandparents to my Son*. It is very possible that this is related to her feelings and experiences as a mother. Her paintings, however, have still maintained that very distinctive Dedron style, that freedom, casualness, beauty and openness. This must be why so many people love her works.

DANGSEL DAWA

Member of the Lhasa Artist's Association; once an art teacher at the Lhasa Children's Palace; pursued advanced studies at the Zhejiang Art College and at the thangka painting class of Tibet University; studied two years of traditional thangka painting, during which she systematically studied traditional ethnic art; found her own entry point to a style that keeps up with contemporary trends, but that does not compromise traditional art; her work has been exhibited many times at fine art, photography and calligraphy exhibitions in Lhasa.

Her painting styles are varied and very difficult to classify. Her various artistic periods have produced their very own different styles and patterns. This may be related to her experience; she used to work as an art teacher at the Lhasa's Children's Palace, a kindergarten teacher and a civil servant. Later, she quit her government job and became a professional artist. As a single mother, she plunged into the sea of entrepreneurship and even had her own bar, bookshop and ceramics art shop. She has experienced a lot. But she never gave up painting and drawing. She says that she is most happy when she is in her studio painting. That is when she can forget all her worries and concentrate; it is like meditation.

She smiled and said, "Those who can paint are the happiest people." The *Mask* series that is part of our exhibition makes a gloomy colour in front of my eyes turn bright; she simply uses pure colours, which makes us feel that her artworks have a lot of potential. She likes to paint masks whose expressions are unambiguous, allowing us to directly see a person's emotions. She said that she does not like painting real people's faces because she has no way of telling what actually lies behind a facial expression, "Only a person's real face would be a genuine mask". I remember this sentence deeply.

An artist's career always splits into an early and a later period. I prefer the later period. Because of my experience, I believe that Dangsel Dawa's paintings are at an early stage and that they are yet to blossom during her most brilliant period.

Left: Dangsel Dawa
Right: A painting from the *Mask* series

TSERING LHAMO

Graduated from Shanghai Theatrical Institute with degrees in stage art and costume design and make-up design; now works as a second grade national costume artist for the Tibetan Autonomous Region dance ensemble; oil painting is her hobby; her painting Potala Palace *was selected for a contemporary Tibetan art exhibition in Japan; her oil painting* The Autumn Field *was selected for the 8th National Art Exhibition.*

She has never regarded herself as a professional painter. Even though she graduated from the Shanghai Theatrical Institute and has obtained excellent professional training, she prefers to regard artistic production as a relaxing leisure activity. Over the past few years, her main activities revolved around her family and work life. All of the costume design of the entire Tibet Autonomous Region's dance ensemble rests on her shoulders. She also has to take care of her own stage art costumes studio. But she still cannot give up painting.

Whenever she has time, she hides away in her studio to paint a few strokes. But she probably never thought about doing this for some purpose. She said that she really does not want to turn what she loves so much into something that has a special use.

But even though she does not want to become a professional painter, she also says that she will probably keep painting for the rest of her life. This is because painting has already become an integral part of her life. Everyone says that the best way to destroy a hobby is by turning it into a profession. In this respect, Tsering Lhamo is really fortunate.

Above: Tsering Lhamo
Right: Silly Little Girl, oil painting

NYEDRON

Graduated with distinction from the University of the Arts in London in fashion photography and design; during her studies, her photographs made it into several fashion and art magazines in the UK and in Europe; after graduating in 2015, she returned home and registered the Holy Mountain Photography Co. Ltd. in Lhasa; in 2016, Nyedron signed a contract with the London-based art gallery Art Represent and some of her works were sold; after returning to Lhasa, Nyedron published her work in several fashion magazines in Tibet and Hong Kong.

She is the only artist at this exhibition who uses photography as a mode of expression. She is also the youngest among the five. What is the unique perspective of a Tibetan girl who was born in the 1990s and who returned from abroad? This is what I am interested in.

Tibet is a hotspot for photographers; but most pictures show the holy mountains and rivers and the vast grasslands or the beautiful Tibetan girls or the elderly herdsmen who are devout Buddhists; I call this the "Shangri-la perspective". These photographers think about lighting effects, precision and the atmosphere of the vast plateau. But these people never think about the actual situation and feelings of the people they photograph; they simply keep reinforcing their image of Tibet.

Nyedron, on the other hand, looks at a Tibet under modernisation. She captures the collision between external cultural elements like LV bags, Coca-Cola or Versace glasses and traditional culture; loss and restructuring, rebellion and conservatism, these are the things that make up Nyedron's visual discourse. A different but certainly existent Tibet.

Above: Nyedron
Right: Modernising the World's Roof,
photograph

DOLMA TSERING: TIBET'S YOUNGEST PRINCIPAL CELLIST ON HER 20 YEAR LONG MUSICAL JOURNEY

7 August 2017

The first time I came into contact with a musical instrument was at the age of seven. It was a toy instrument sold for five Yuan at a department store in Shigatse. I used it to learn birthday songs. After my parents noticed my love for music, they bought me an electronic keyboard.

My mother was a music teacher for young children, she played the accordion; she also had a notebook that was full of music and lyrics of popular songs at the time. I started learning how to play piano using this notebook and then also participated in art groups and performances at primary school.

At the age of 12, as I was about to finish primary school, the Tibet Autonomous Region (TAR) Art School came to Shigatse to recruit new students. I naturally signed up for the examination. Simultaneously, I also passed the exam for inland Tibetan schooling in Chinese areas, because my culture teachers at the time all opposed my choice to study music. But luckily my parents respected my hobby and so I became a cello student at the TAR Art School.

In September 1997, I began to formally study the cello. Every day, I would spend six hours practicing basic skills; six years passed in an instant. When I was able to play some of the pieces that I personally really wanted to play, I realised for the first time how much I loved this instrument.

I remember how at the time, the internet was not as developed as it is today, information was limited and it was tough to communicate with the outside world. We were basically unable to learn about other same-aged cellists from outside Tibet or to find out about what other cello concerts were like.

After I had started studying the cello, the first time I ventured out to see the world was in 2000, when I went to Shanghai to participate in the fourth China Eastern National Cello Competition. I was excited because I had the chance to see so many outstanding cellists, but it was also a very painful experience.

It was because in Tibet I was the best but as soon as I left, I realised that everyone else was so much better; it really hit me, I shed many painful tears.

After the competition, I returned to Tibet and no longer thought of myself as so high and pure. I began to practice a hundred times harder, I focused on higher and farther goals and put all my efforts into learning the cello.

Dolma Tsering playing the cello in Professor Zhu Yibing's cello ensemble named Moonlight, 2015

A daily practice session

That experience was really an important turning point for me, because it encouraged me to not directly start working after finishing Art School, but to continue my studies at a more professional school.

In 2003, I managed to start an undergraduate degree at the Central Conservatory of Music in Beijing, continuing my cello studies; I was the first Tibetan student who entered the Central Conservatory of Music as a cello major.

When I started my studies in Beijing, I realised that many of my classmates had been learning instruments professionally from the age of seven or eight and their technical skills were excellent; I realised that mine weren't sufficient, which once again spurred me to practice even harder.

In my second year, the world famous cellist, Zhu Yibing, returned to China to teach at our school. All of us were very anxious to learn from him. For me, being able to study at university was a rare chance, so I plucked up my courage and directly expressed to him my wish to study under him.

He could more or less sense my sincerity and immediately took me on as his student. The remaining three years at university, studying under Professor Zhu, were the most important ones regarding my musical and artistic education and socialisation. Suddenly, my technique and understanding improved dramatically and I assumed the post of the principal cellist at the Central Conservatory Orchestra for three years.

Zhu Yibing's cello ensemble

After graduation, I joined the TAR Song and Dance Troupe Orchestra and until this day, I remain their youngest principal cellist. In 2009, I entered the Art Institute of Tibet University to study under Professor Gendun Phelgye, and particularly chose to study Tibetan religious music.

I think that regarding art in today's Tibet, music, especially instrumental music, is the weakest field, particularly symphonic orchestral music. This then also touches upon the responsibility of us contemporary professional musicians.

First, there are too few people studying music, which is one direct cause for this deficiency. Second, there are many policies that lead to the drainage of talent and restrict creative thinking. In this sort of environment many people decide to give up on their musical dreams.

The poster for Dolma Tsering's third concert

In July 2017, I held a concert in Lhasa. It was the third time that I performed as a soloist; the previous two times were in July and September 2007 at concerts held in Beijing and Lhasa, respectively. This one was exactly ten years since the first two.

When organising the concert, my original vision was to present the different stages and achievements of my career, but I also hoped to liven up the weak field of instrumental music in Tibet and to enrich Lhasa people's spiritual and cultural lives.

We experimented with many new elements; we mixed together traditional Tibetan and western music, using western instruments to play Tibetan music. The audience loved it. I even heard that the solo piece played on the cello and the *dranyen* made people in the audience shed tears of emotion. For us musicians, this is even more gratifying than applause.

Through this concert, my own goals for the future became much clearer, which is to use western instruments to perform local music. This is my professional dream, this is also my responsibility as a young Tibetan musician.

FROM YOUNG ROCKER TO UNIVERSITY PROFESSOR: AN INTERVIEW WITH TENZIN DAWA FROM THE BAND NAMCHAG

Tsesung Lhamo of Sweet Tea House WeChat channel

18 July 2016

Most people in Lhasa know the band Namchag; they have many loyal fans. Today, we invite the band's founder, Tenzin Dawa, to the Sweet Tea House to talk about his life, his current work, music, society and, of course, about some unavoidable things related to his band…

LIFE

Let's begin by talking a bit about your current work and living situation.

At the moment I am mainly teaching undergraduate and postgraduate students at the Art Institute of Tibet University, while also doing some related research. In terms of living situation, well, I have to take care of both my aging parents and my children. There is a lot going on in a big family, it's very fulfilling. When I am free, I also like to drive to different places by myself to experience and record the situation of people and the environment in times of societal change; I also use this opportunity to collect and learn some folk music and to produce some experimental music.

If we had to pick the central themes of your life, we could certainly not do without 'music'. As far as I know, you graduated from the music academy of Minzu University of China, so what I would like to know is whether this was just some coincidence or whether you chose this career for your love for music and pursued this goal to become a musician all along?

My parents were artists and there was always an artistic atmosphere at home, which really influenced me and made me love art, particularly music. In terms of the life choices I made, music always played a role. I can say that from my time at the Tibetan Art School to being a student in Beijing, and to working at the Art Institute of Tibet University, including completing my Masters degree in between, I have always been really lucky in that my journey in pursuit of an artistic career has been a very smooth one. If one were to place all of the world's subjects in front of me and make me choose one, I would still, without any doubt, pick music. The saying that "a person who manages to do what he or she dreamt of doing as a child is a happy person" really applies to me. Music helps you understand many innermost feelings that script or words simply cannot express; it is that feeling that "you can only sense intuitively, but cannot put into words". Even if I spend day and night listening to music, writing

music, singing or playing instruments, I never feel tired or exhausted. When one loves something this much, one has no regrets. But of course, all of this is also inseparable from the immense support and understanding that I have experienced from my family.

After you graduated from Minzu University, apart from teaching at Tibet University, you also opened the Unplugged Music Bar in Lhasa, what was the main intention behind this?

Yes, the reasons why I called the bar Unplugged are twofold; firstly, it simply means that people perform without amplifying their music, and second, on a deeper level, it is about returning to more simplistic and original aesthetics. I wanted to emphasise the pure and genuine spirit of music and thus draw attention to the importance of caring for our lives and existence. But I realised that this original idea was really just an idea because in reality, most people today only get excited by amplified music. So we were forced to use 'plugged' music to convey the message of 'unplugged' music. In any case, our bar attracted many people who, apart from having a good time, were also exposed to the diversity of international and local music culture. Our stage was open to anyone who could play an instrument or sing, they could simply go up and perform. It then slowly turned into a platform for professional and amateur musicians to express themselves, communicate and learn from each other. So, in a sense, the bar became the musical platform to bring together different musicians that I had always wanted to establish. Finally, considering that Lhasa had no official music shops or private music schools, I later extended the bar into the Sacred Music Shop and the Sacred Music School.

NAMCHAG

Most people actually know you through the band Namchag. Being part of this band must have been an extraordinarily exciting time in your life; as the band's 'soul', could you tell us more about how you came to found this group?

When I was at Minzu University I would often go to the Minzu Song and Dance Ensemble to watch Cui Jian and Tengger rehearse. I also went to the newly opened Midi School of Music to audit classes, which is when I first thought about forming a band. When I returned from Beijing, I realised that in the streets and alleys of Lhasa, where people would sing and dance, most music that was played was foreign. That was when I decided to write songs that were not simply about the "blue sky and white clouds, beauty and gratefulness" and that only talked about love; I wanted to write music that would reflect the darker sides of human beings and society, that would express people's deepest worries, struggles, contradictions and pains. Since rock music is one of the straightest and simplest forms to express these kinds of feelings, I chose to do rock music. When I was running Unplugged I met a few guys who came over to play and we got along quite well, so we formed a band.

When we looked for a name, there were three factors that mattered to me: first, it had to be timely; second, it had to be Tibetan; third, it had to have a deep and acute meaning. One day as I was walking along Barkhor, I came across the word *phurba* (ཕུར་པ་ - a ritual dagger, also called *namchag*) and I immediately knew that this would be the name of our band. For one, from an artistic perspective, the structure of the word is quite avantgarde and unique; plus, it exudes distinct Tibetan characteristics; and most importantly, it has more profound implications, conquering the demons, attacking the darkness and evil, exactly what I wanted to express with my music; this is how the name *Namchag* came about.

Because most of the members were mere amateurs and not professionally trained musicians, we started off by listening to a lot of outstanding national and international music, while at the same time also collecting and listening to traditional Tibetan music. During that time, I wrote the songs *Dream Girl, Rinzin Wangmo, Some People, White, Wheel of Time,* etc. At the beginning, it was me who wrote most of the songs, but slowly, when we made our second album, the other members would also write music, which was a huge improvement.

You were one of the first Tibetan rock bands. Subsequently, popular music began to grow in Tibet and many music and rock lovers also started to release their own records. We can say that you were successful pioneers. About your band's style and concept, you once said that your music is penetrating, not only expressing the good things in life, but also the other side of humans and society. Looking back, how would you evaluate your band and your music?

Today, the main feeling when thinking back is that we were not very mature in many ways, but not being mature can also be positive. When we were young we were full of passion, we were genuine and not out for fame and profit, we just wanted to express some of our ideas through rock music. I actually think that the young and frivolous attitude is ideal for rock music. While praising the beauty of life on the one hand, we could attack the dark sides of humans and society on the other. Looking back, I think that we had a positive impact upon society at the time. We did quite well. At least many young people listened to our music and starting paying attention to themselves and to society, they started to reflect. Reflecting is in itself the beginning of change, even if one does not change directly, when one starts reflecting, things are already starting to become very different; it is like sowing a seed of change and one will start to subconsciously generate self-awareness and thus break free from ignorance.

Music must be beautiful, the vast majority of music starts from this premise to express beauty, while often neglecting the ugly side; our band tried to convey beauty by fighting against the ugly. It is a bit like when you really love something, you will most likely not ignore its shortcomings, so we always tried to point out what was bad, hoping to thus improve things. It is exactly like the idiom "loyal advice jars on the ears".

But if I were to start a band at my age now, it would be different from back then, because one needs to think about and consider many different aspects, for example, the aesthetics of music itself, the messages that one wants to convey with one's music, the form and angle of expression as well as the aesthetic level, orientation, understanding of and impact upon one's audience. Back then we were young and without much to worry about, we followed the mantra "if you like it take it, if not then leave it". It was a "just do it" attitude.

We have not heard much about Namchag over the past few years, could you let us know a bit more about what has been going on?

As with all things, you get together and you part, there is a beginning and there is an end; a band is no exception. I always hoped that the band would be able to transform itself on the level of music, to constantly make breakthroughs, to move forward along with the changes happening in society itself. I want to see music and messages developing as we accumulate experience and to avoid stagnating at a simple, premature level. I also don't like to see bands merely becoming simply tool for rock music amusement on a commercial level, this is not what I want to see and it is not what those who really like Namchag want to see. Before we split up, I said to the other members, "I'd rather die than become corrupted". Not long ago, namely in December 2013, all the band members signed an agreement promising not to use the name Namchag to engage in any performances; after that we announced the end of the band.

I know the band belongs to the past, but as a fan, could I ask you to share with your many fans some anecdotes or other unforgettable events in the history of the band?

For me, most of the interesting things happened when the band initially started off. That was the happiest time, we all felt passionate and had no interest in fame and profit. None of us had families yet and we got along really well. I remember when we first started, we rented a rehearsal room; once we were rehearsing for a long time when suddenly there was a power cut. We only found out later that it was our neighbours who got angry because of the noise and cut the electricity cable. Subsequently, we had to cover doors and windows with blankets and other things to make the room sound-proof. Another time we went out for some food and when we came back, we realised all our things had been stolen, so we went to purchase everything again and continued to practice. There were so many such little anecdotes back then. But the most unforgettable event was when we attended the 2005 Midi Festival in Beijing; it was the first time that a Tibetan band was invited for their artistic value and not for some commercial reasons. Attending this rock music festival under the theme of "Saving China's Rivers" was really a milestone.

So, did you ever consider staying in Beijing to develop your musical career as a band?

We did have that opportunity; but we had our own careers, the band was always just a hobby, it was never a proper job for us. Turning a band into a professional career would have involved overcoming many challenges, which is why we returned. In fact, I suddenly remembered another anecdote, do you want to hear it?

Of course

We were once invited by a *nangma* club (a Tibetan dance hall) to give a concert. We were a bit drunk when we were on stage, when a strong Chinese guy came up to us. We initially thought that he wanted to cheer and drink with us, but he actually came up and grabbed our bass player, saying "stop right now, it's unbearable!" We had no idea what to do, whether to get off stage or whether to continue to perform. That guy was either drunk, or he simply disliked our music, or maybe his girlfriend was too interested in us guys. Just joking (laughs)...

MUSIC

Regardless of whether it was with Namchag or in your current job as an educator, you have always been involved with traditional folk music. Some people have criticised you for modernising traditional music and combining it with rock music, saying that you "insulted traditional ethnic music". But it is indisputable that you opened up new possibilities for traditional music and made it accessible to young people. Where do you currently see a market for traditional music?

In our music, we had a couple of traditional songs with rock influences, but they never lost their original characteristics; you could always immediately tell it is a Tibetan song and this is what is really important. Of course, looking back now, there were some obvious shortcomings and I truly hope that there will be others who will do better than us in maintaining the traditional characteristics of a piece, while at the same time being innovative. Maintaining continuity in change is a problem and a challenge that every single artist encounters. As far as I can see, common music in Tibet faces two situations: on the one hand, you have the *nangma* clubs that focus on folk music but lack an understanding of the diversity of contemporary music, so they often simply produce disco editions of folk songs, which is possibly the simplest and most practical way of entertainment. On the other hand, you have the young urbanites, especially those who studied in China; their world-view is much broader, they are familiar with Chinese music scenes and western music, but they lack an understanding of local folk music, to the point that we find no traditional Tibetan aesthetic 'genes' in their music at all. I truly hope that these two groups can merge and find a common language to reconcile the traditional and the modern, the native and the foreign. If you can find such a common angle, there will be a new market for traditional music.

As for audiences, we do also need some slightly more picky people who don't just follow the mainstream. At the moment, most music lovers stagnate at an entertainment level, they are not well-versed when it comes to an understanding of other levels in music, such as heritage, education, expression, etc. Music is evidently more than just entertainment, it is an essential part of people's lives. So I just hope that audiences will become a bit more open-minded and don't just consume music for the sake of enjoyment.

What are your views on the contemporary Tibetan music scene? Are there any singers or bands that you like?

Honestly, I am a little bit disappointed about the current situation. Firstly, most of today's music is simply an imitation of foreign music; secondly, even though there are many pieces that claim to be Tibetan, in terms of structure and harmony they are completely alienated from the original characteristics of Tibetan music. For instance, sometimes blues songs are equipped with Tibetan lyrics and then presented as new Tibetan music. I feel that many people don't even understand this anymore, especially young people who have no sense or feeling for traditional characteristics. Tibetan lyrics don't make a Tibetan song, Tibetan music is defined by its distinctive melody, rhythm and structure. It is the responsibility of musicians to make sure that we don't accidentally destroy traditional Tibetan music through this so-called new Tibetan music.

I hope that those who make traditional Tibetan music will go back to its pure roots, without replacing its original tonal structure with common harmonies. The essence of traditional music must not be compromised, or else don't call it Tibetan music and thus obscure the facts. If we don't stick to our heritage and the unique features of Tibetan music, we simply borrow from other people at the expense of losing our own traditions. In some sense, this is indeed one musical choice, but if this becomes the mainstream way, then we have a problem and one day you get to the point of no return, and you will suddenly realise that you are no longer yourself.

Nowadays, we rarely encounter traditional Tibetan music, including court music, religious music, folk music or opera, as a whole. It is ok to simply get together, form a band and play music. But I hope that it won't just be about entertainment, about being cool and following the trend. I hope that people will reflect as to whether what they do is useful, whether their music has value. I also hope that on the basis of our own traditional music, we go and borrow from other people's music, not in a clumsy copy-cat fashion, but in an intelligent way. Of course, all bands go through a stage when they copy their idols, but copying must not become a goal in itself, you cannot always stay in the shadow of someone else. You should also not be overly proud of some minor successes, but work hard in trying to find your own ways and style to express traditional Tibetan music.

So, honestly, apart from Choying Dolma (who strictly speaking isn't even a singer), there is no one I particularly enjoy. Sometimes I like someone, but then they quickly change and become worse. Society has become extremely impatient, that's the way it is.

Have you ever thought of going back and getting involved again?

I really enjoy my current situation, it makes no difference whether I come back or not. Now, I just want to peacefully make the music that I like, want to use the music that I like to express what is going on at the grassroots level of society and in the minds of the people. There is too much boisterous music out there today, no need for me to get involved and join in the excitement.

Finally, is there anything that you would like to say to those youngsters who like music and specifically rock music?

First of all, you should all listen to various, different kinds of traditional music, and don't just try and understand the lyrics, the religious or spiritual meanings. Try to also understand the special characteristics and profound emotions inherent in the musical structure themselves as well as the artistic aesthetics and 'genes'. Apart from that, you should also listen to music from other groups around the globe, and particularly music that fits your personality.

I hope that today's musicians won't be too obsessed with fame and profit or get too carried away by trivial things. Why did bands like The Beatles or U2 become so famous? It is because they touched upon themes that are of interest to all human beings; they pursued things like truth, equality, freedom and peace. Today, we often simply look at ourselves, are only concerned about our own little universe, but that is not good, there is no value in that; the ultimate goal of art should be to change people for the better. We must pay more attention to what happens around us, for instance, our culture of compassion, our love for all people. We can start from the details in our own immediate society to convey and touch upon larger issues; that would be ideal.

Another piece of advice is to not simply use, for instance, the harmonies and structures of hip hop, equip them with Tibetan lyrics and then call it new Tibetan music. In this way, we will actually deceive those who don't understand music. Finally, you should also learn to be more patient, you should calm down, read some books and pay attention to producing good music.

In that way you won't lose your own characteristics or the characteristics of your own local music. You will also find a suitable way to express yourself in today's world; that would indeed be a good solution.

Thank you for sharing so many thoughts with us, it was a pleasure talking with you.

I thank Sweet Tea House.